MW01089322

MIGUEL QUINTANA PALI

X U E Ñ O S

THE STORY OF THE DREAMS BEHIND XCARET, THE BEST PARK IN THE WORLD

conecta
MÉXICO

The paper used in the production of this book is made from wood grown in forests and plantations managed following the highest environmental standards, thus ensuring the environmentally sustainable exploitation of these natural resources, for the benefit of people. Dreams.

Penguin
Random House
Grupo Editorial

Xueños
The Story of the Dreams behind Xcaret, the Best Park in the World

Originally published in Spanish as *Xueños. La historia detrás de Xcaret, el mejor parque del mundo*

Second edition published in English by Penguin Random House Grupo Editorial: January, 2021
First reprint: February, 2022
Second reprint: November, 2022
Third reprint: March, 2023

Thanks to life, my perfect dream

«*A master in the art of life makes no distinction between work and play: work and leisure, mind and body, education and recreation, love and religion; he can hardly tell them apart. He simply pursues perfection in everything he does; he leaves it to others to decide whether he is working or playing. In his mind, he is always doing both.*»

ZEN BUDDHIST SAYING

CONTENTS

COMING SOON...

WHY TALK
WHEN I CAN SING?

Let me share with you the songs that have accompanied
me along my adventures. Find my playlist "Xueños"
in Spotify with this code:

WARNING!

The names of our first parks begin with
the letter «X», so we decided to name
the newer ones in a similar fashion.
Nowadays, that «X» is rooted in our
vocabulary, it is part of our essence, so
you will find it used proudly in words
throughout this book.

INTRODUCTION

To dream is to visualize a great idea in action.

I live my dreams three times: first, I imagine them; then, I make them come true; and finally, I remember them. That's how I have managed to live life thrice—the best formula for longevity.

I have xperienced my moments of greatest clarity in my sleep: dreaming in color about xperiences beyond my knowledge, my understanding, my life xperiences, my education; designing and explaining the intricate workings of a complex system of industrial production that is way ahead of its time. Many times I've had these incredible dreams, and about many such systems, and upon waking up I have come to the inevitable conclusion that, in our daily lives, we are far from being able to exploit our mind's full potential—just as artificial intelligence is far from catching up with humans. Just how many human advances may have been created this way, springing spontaneously one night from humans' intelligent subconscious?

I have also had fantastic dreams in which I fly, or rather, in which I jump around: I take a huge leap, and just before reaching the floor, I leap a little higher up, and then again, going higher each time, and faster. I've traveled all over the world this way, taking a bird's eye view from the silent heights, feeling the wind on my skin. You have to learn to have nice dreams, or to wake up just in time.

If God were to grant me an impossible dream, I would ask for a cat's seven lives, and to be able to fly and sing like a nightingale. Still, I have had most of my dreams while awake, I have pursued them, and I have reached almost all of them. Even dreaming must be learned if we want to be more than simple Dreamers.

The dreamer's counterpart is the entrepreneur, the doer, the one who makes dreams come true. Only three steps are required:

1. Write down your dream on a piece of paper and set a deadline to transform it into an *objective*.
2. Break your objective down into small steps to make it into a *plan*.
3. Back your plan up with actions so that it becomes a *reality*.

Life is the color and the taste of your dreams. This is the tasty and colorful dream I am living.

MIGUEL PALI QUINTANA PALI

FIRST **HALF**

SO LUCKY
TO HAVE BEEN BORN!

CHAPTER 1

I am the founder and General Director of Grupo Xcaret, but first and foremost I am Miguel Pali Quintana Pali. I was born on September 2, 1946, in Boston, Massachusetts, where my father was studying an MBA at Harvard University. I am the second child in a family of six children. Although we were all born in different countries—Chile, the United States, and Mexico—when we came of age, we all followed our hearts and chose to be Mexican. As the song by Alberto Cortez says: «I'm so lucky to have been born!»

My father, Carlos Quintana Gómez-Daza, came from a family in Puebla. He had graduated as an electrical and mechanical engineer from the Escuela Superior de Ingeniería Mecánica y Eléctrica (ESIME) in Mexico's National Polytechnic Institute. He was studying industrial engineering at Columbia University, in New York, when he met my mother, Lulu Pali

Solomon, a music student from Hawaii at the same university. It was love at first sight! They got married in March 1944, only a few months after they first met.

Soon after, they moved to Mexico City, where Carlos, my eldest brother, was born. However, they later relocated to Boston so my father could earn his master's degree. That's where I was born followed by my sister Rosi, soon after, once we had moved back to Mexico City my sister Lulu was born.

In 1950, my father was sent to Santiago, Chile, to work for the United Nations' Economic Commission for Latin America (ECLA), known today as the Economic Commission for Latin America and the Caribbean (ECLAC). We lived there for ten years, and it was during that time that our youngest siblings, Lupe and Santi, were born, completing the set of male and female pairs born in every country where our family lived.

All of us children were given a Hispanic first name and a Hawaiian middle name: Carlos Kaukaha, Miguel Pali—my parents were so creative that they used my mother's surname as my middle name—, Rosita Leinaala, Lulu Ululani, Ernesto Santiago Dominicus Hotu-Matua, and Guadalupe Pauahi. And all bearing our paternal and maternal surnames, Quintana Pali.

Although I was born in my mother's country, I took my father's nationality and even did national military service when I turned 18. Don't forget: We Mexicans are born *wherever it damn well pleases us*!

My father had a split-personality: most of the time he had a big smile and was cheerful, polite, and kind; but at work he was always serious and formal. He was an outstanding engineer, well-known in Latin America, an expert in bio-cellulose, among other industrial matters, which led him to occupy important positions, both in the Mexican public administration—as General Director for Credit at Nacional

Financiera (NAFIN), Mexico's development bank—and in the United Nations' offices in Santiago—as ECLA's Executive Secretary. He was always impeccably dressed, like any good government official and diplomat. I remember him shining his shoes and changing his white shirt with its starched collar whenever my parents attended some dinner. He traveled a lot because he had to visit every Latin American country, as well as the UN's headquarters in New York. Every time he made a trip, he brought a small souvenir for all six of us. Despite living abroad for so many years, he was always passionately in love with his country.

However, he had a bohemian side. At home he had a 9-track recorder where he would record a song, playing an instrument to one audio channel, then he would record the same song, playing another instrument to another audio channel, and so on, practically creating his own orchestra. He even brought a marimba from Chiapas, Mexico, into Santiago, Chile, and taught himself to play. He composed his own songs and sang and played the guitar by ear. My parents played four-handed duets on two grand pianos, «His» and «Hers», both of which are still at my parents' house. My father was the life and soul of parties, he had a great sense of humor, he loved to tell jokes and play pranks. He always filled our home with joy. I inherited his good humor, his love of music, and his love for Mexico.

My mother, on the other hand, was the serious parent, the strict one, the one who brought us down to earth, an essential part of our upbringing. I remember how embarrassing it was when, at parties, she asked the four eldest children to dance the hula with her. Hawaiian by birth, and later an American—Hawaii was an American territory, but in 1959 it became the 50th and last state to join the United States— she always spoke to us in English and it was in English that she told us off, and though my siblings and I spoke Spanish among ourselves, we understood her perfectly.

Hawaiian Wedding Song - Alfred Apaka

In Hawaii, everything revolves around nature. In each of the five houses we lived in while growing up there was a beautiful garden, created and cared for by my mother. Later on, when we all went back to live in Mexico City for good, she created her own orchid garden with species from all over the country. She would sort the trash and make her own compost. She taught us to consume only what was necessary and to respect our environment. We inherited her sense of formality, but also the awe of nature that lived deep in her heart.

SANTIAGO, CHILE

I arrived in Chile when I was four, so my earliest memories are of a very pleasant life in Santiago. Every morning we would get up very early, because all of us had kids' chores which we would take turns doing. While some prepared oatmeal for breakfast, others set the table, and the oldest children—Carlos and I—would usually go and buy milk from a horse-drawn milk wagon, parked at the corner of our street. Afterwards, we would make our beds, before setting off for school, walking about four blocks to the corner where we would take the bus.

Our mother taught us to be mindful about money and to manage it. She had a notebook where she kept a record of how well we had fulfilled our chores: whether we had left our clothes lying on the floor, made our beds properly, or helped with breakfast. She would award us points or take them away. We would collect points, and during the weekend buy pencils or erasers. On Sundays, she would also give us a small allowance, which was determined by our behavior. She would reward us by giving us enough to satisfy our basic needs plus a little bit more to buy ice cream or some rolled wafers— «barquillos»—after church.

Even though we lived in Santiago, on weekends we always visited the coast or the mountain ranges, usually staying at my parents' Chilean friends' country houses. During our longer holidays, we used to go south to the lakes. It was from these xperiences, I'm sure, that my love of natural scenery was born. Chile, in those days, was completely isolated from the rest of the world. We had no close relatives over there, but we used to call all my father's work colleagues «aunties» and «uncles» because they truly were our only family over there. At ECLA, there were representatives from all over Latin America, so half of our adopted aunties and uncles were Chilean, while the other half came from the rest of the continent.

As a UN official and a foreign diplomat, my father could take advantage of a work benefit that allowed him and all the family to go back home on vacation every other year, a home leave. So, every two years, we would return to Mexico City to visit our grandparents, uncles and cousins. Sometimes, we would also travel to Hawaii to spend time with our maternal grandparents, who still lived there.

At one point, we moved to my mother's homeland for an entire year. That is why I ended up repeating fifth grade, once in Santiago and a second time in Honolulu, at Liholiho, a public school close to my grandparents' home. Meanwhile, my father remained at his job, going back and forth between Hawaii and Chile. One of the things I always remember about Hawaii is that people used to go barefoot. Not wearing shoes except when at work is a custom, not a sign of poverty or austerity. At my grandparents' house, visitors left their shoes (if they wore any) just outside the door, Japanese style. The problem with being half Hawaiian is that every time someone comes to see me at my office, I have to dash to find and put on the shoe I've discarded.

That time in Hawaii was like a sabbatical year during which we interrupted our studies in Chile. These xperiences were part of our parents' plans to raise us multiculturally.

MEXICO CITY

My father was offered a job in Mexico City, at Nacional Financiera, a federal government development bank, first as an industrial programming manager and, years later, as the person in charge of starting the Multilateral Investment Fund (FOMIN), so we returned from Chile in 1960.

I joined the Boy Scouts, just as I had done in Hawaii. With them, I went camping all around the country, I hitchhiked across Mexico, and I learned the principles of what today we call «sustainability», trying to minimize the impact on nature when setting up a campsite and learning to interact with her. This ethical foundation, alongside the core values I learned at home, were key in my development.

In 1963, I left home to study high school at the Tecnológico de Monterrey, at its Monterrey campus. Back then, high school studies took two years, not three, like today. I had to stay in Monterrey for two summers to get ahead in my coursework and finish high school in only three semesters— which I did, with honors. I had been in a serious relationship for five years and I was desperate to get through my courses so that I could finish university and get married.

Besides knowledge, what I most value today about my studies away from home was living with others. Initially, I lived at Tec de Monterrey's boarding house. Afterwards, I rented an apartment with some of my classmates and my brother Carlos. The projects we worked on together in class and living in the same space taught us how to work as a team.

I decided to continue my studies at the Tec de Monterrey and started a bachelor's degree in Chemical Engineering. However, I only stayed there for a year. Even though I enjoyed it, I was not too keen on the focus on science and research, so I switched to Architecture at Universidad Iberoamericana (Ibero) in Mexico City.

After three years at Ibero I decided to leave, in part because the academic level was not demanding enough, and also because teachers' absences were constant and on the rise. I felt that staying there was a waste of time. I was getting rusty.

«DON'T LET SCHOOLING INTERFERE WITH YOUR EDUCATION.»

MARK TWAIN

In 1967, my father was asked to serve the UN once again, now as ECLA's Executive Secretary, in Santiago. My parents lived there until 1973. This time, instead of moving with their six children, they decided to leave us on our own in our home in the Lomas de Chapultepec neighborhood. Back then, Lupe was 12, Santi was 15, Lulu was 18, Rosi was 19, I was 20, and Carlos was 22. A cook and a cleaning lady helped us out with the housework. Lulu, the fourth child, was the one in charge of the house. My mother had trusted her enough to add her signature to the checkbook, so she paid for all services and tuition fees, and on Saturdays she would go to local markets—La Merced and San Juan—with my two other sisters to buy our food for the week. On her way to the university—Universidad Nacional Autónoma de México (UNAM)—she would drop my two youngest siblings, who were in junior high and high school, at their school, Escuela Moderna Americana, in the Del Valle neighborhood. In the afternoon, they would take the city bus to get back home.

Tierra mestiza - Gerardo Tamez

«SEEKING YOUNG, INTELLIGENT, AMBITIOUS PEOPLE...»

Before leaving for Chile, my father asked a NAFIN director for a favor: to take me in as his assistant and to serve as my mentor. So, while studying at Ibero, I also worked at NAFIN in the afternoons. My job was to translate articles and reports from Spanish to English and vice versa. My first translations were awful, but I learned to use the dictionary and became a fast translator. I did that for about two years, until the first computers were brought into management. It was around that time that I was invited to work in NAFIN's Organizational division, and later the Computing department.

Shortly after, while looking for a job, I came across an ad in the classified ads section of *Excélsior* newspaper. I still remember it clearly: «Seeking young, intelligent, ambitious people. Earn MX $1,500-2,000, depending on skills.» I applied and they hired me as a computer programmer with the highest salary offered, which quite pleased me. Two years later, I was the company's manager.

The company was called Computadoras y Sistemas and its offices where in the Industrial Vallejo neighborhood. The proprietor also owned *ingenios*—sugar cane mills—in Veracruz, so we had to develop programs to pay the mill workers, to lend money to the cane growers to plant their own crops and to do their book-keeping, to pay the freighters transporting the cane, and to do the payroll. Every Friday, someone drove from Veracruz to Mexico City to bring the week's information, and we worked through the night to process it. We then informed the bank how much money would be needed and the payroll was sent on a light aircraft first thing on Saturday morning to pay the sugar cane field workers near Córdoba city in Veracruz.

With time, one learns the tricks in every trade. For instance, the sugar cane cutters who owed money to one mill would avoid selling their product to that mill so that the payment would not be discounted from their debt. Instead, they would sell it to another neighboring one, to which they owed nothing. This way, they prevented their creditors from collecting the money owed. As for the freighters, they would submerge their sugar cane loaded carts in the river, so that the cane would absorb water and weigh more when placed on the scale. Carts were weighed before and after being unloaded, and the difference in weight determined the payment. Mexican ingenuity beat the *ingenio*'s wit.

Canción mexicana - Aida Cuevas

THE DAWN
OF AN ENTREPRENEUR

CHAPTER 2

I was always interested in business, and I took my first steps in Chile. When my mother gave me money to buy pencils and erasers, I would buy one box of each: I was already thinking about wholesale, and about who I could resell them to. At home we had large gardens, since back then we were on the outskirts of the city—nowadays, this area is considered to be in the city center—and next to our house was a cherry orchard and some pens. I had my own chickens and I would sell their eggs to my mother, to whom I would also offer to mow the lawn for a reasonable fee.

Every week, my mother would go to Librería Americana de Santiago, a bookstore that sold American magazines, including *The Saturday Evening Post*, a family magazine in English that my mother used to purchase and which she would give to me after reading. I remember always finding an ad about a moving company, Mayflower, and other ads depicting various car brands. I would use scissors to carefully cut out every picture of a vehicle and play with them, pretending I had fleets of moving trucks and rental cars made of paper.

In those days, there were practically no toys in Chile, so those cutouts from the magazines where my toys. I remember a trip to Mexico when we went to the first Sears store at the corner of Insurgentes Avenue and San Luis Potosí Street, in the Roma Sur neighborhood. I kept going back to stare at a small truck whose tailgate could open. My mother noticed my behavior and asked me if I liked it. When I told her that I liked it a lot, she bought it for me. That was my first toy, around the age of ten.

Once, as a child, I got some expensive caramel and pecan sweets for my birthday, the kind you wouldn't easily find at any store around the corner. The next day, I took a lid from a cardboard shoe box, hung it around my neck with a piece of thin rope, put the sweets on top, and went out to sell them to the construction workers at a building site next to my house. I had no idea about prices, so I ended up asking for too little, considering their real cost. I sold all of them at once, many of them on credit, since construction workers got paid on the weekends. Come Saturday, almost no one paid their debt, but I still thought I had done the best business deal ever.

When I was in elementary school, spinning tops and marbles were popular. For a time, at recess, I would bring in a shoe box into which I had cut some small holes with numbers above each one. Then, I would draw a line on the floor some distance away from the box. My classmates would kneel at this line and shoot their marbles: if any went into one of the holes, they would win the number of marbles marked on the hole; otherwise, if their marble didn't get into any of the holes, I got to keep it. Since most could not hit the target, I accumulated the marbles, which I would later sell back to them so they could keep playing. It was a good business, until someone at school realized that I was running some type of home-made casino and they forbade it. Other little businesses I had going on included selling my sandwich, exchanging lunches, organizing raffles, selling my old textbooks, and many more. I even used to rent chewing gum in all sorts of flavors, which came from the US: the newer the gum, the greater the flavor and higher the price.

When I got to junior high, back in Mexico, I devoted myself to making balsa wood crucifixes, which I assembled inside bottles of Pisco, a Peruvian grape spirit. I carved each piece using sharp cutters, I decorated them, and then I carefully introduced them through the bottle's mouth and stuck them together with drops of white glue. I remember encouraging my parents to have more parties at home so they would drink more Pisco, since these were the only bottles I could use because of their flat bottoms. By selling these bottled crucifixes I *supported myself* all through junior high.

During these early years, summers were always busy. In Chile, I used to go camping. In Mexico, I worked on a construction project at Presa Infernillo, an embankment dam on the Balsas river. I also worked in the Paseo de las Palmas' interchange, when they built Mexico City's outer beltway, the Periférico; and a couple of times, when I was in senior high school, I worked at a petrochemical plant in the U.S. with one of my father's acquaintances.

I was always searching for something that could make me a profit and always had the mind of a merchant, I have thought like a grownup ever since I was a child: I was very formal, very earnest, very responsible. I remember a ping-pong tournament in sixth grade. I was nowhere near winning one of the first places, but I did beat a major opponent, who was older than me and very skilled. I said to myself: «Look,

Miguel, you've beaten this guy. You deserve a reward.» I took out some money from my piggy bank and bought myself some ice cream. My brother Carlos would spend the allowance my mother gave us on Sundays on his bike; I, on the other hand, would save mine, but on that day I felt I deserved a reward.

Looking back, I think I was always industrious, thrifty and frugal. These days I might invest millions alongside my partners in projects or in company properties, but I still manage every single one of my expenses minutely, including the most basic daily ones. I don't think I will ever live like a rich man, it's too expensive and time-consuming.

At first, one starts buying a small thing to resell for profit. Later, investments become a little bigger. When I was a young man, some of my classmates got their hands on some cars, fixed them, and then resold them to buy better ones. I did something different.

When I was studying at Tec de Monterrey, all of us students who came from other states went home for long weekends and holidays. We had to book tickets in advance with the only two bus companies available, Transportes Anáhuac and Transportes del Norte. Inevitably, there were always people who weren't able to get tickets, so I started chartering buses. I gathered all my Sunday allowances and hired a bus to pick people up at Tec's boarding house at five o'clock, just after lunch, on a given day. I put up photocopied flyers everywhere saying: «Bus to Mexico City, at such a price, on such day, at such a time, tickets sold at 'La Ratonera' boarding house, room X, from 7 to 10 in the evening.» For starters, I saved my classmates the taxi fare to the bus terminal and their trip to buy the tickets. As the departure day got closer, I still had not sold a single ticket, since everyone waited until the last minute. In the end, the bus I had hired sold out, and it became clear that I needed more than one bus, so the second time, I chartered two buses, and then three. Some people would buy half a ticket, because they would travel standing if there were no more seats available, or because they would get off halfway to Mexico City, in San Luis Potosí. That was a profitable business, which by the time I left the Tec had become so necessary to students that I passed it on to Association of Mexico City Students, and it became their main source of income for their events.

When I returned to the capital in 1967, after my parents had gone to live to Chile, I bought 10 chinchillas, small rodents with very fine coats, up to 90 hairs per follicle. I gathered cement mix, bought structural tubes and roofing sheets, and made a small shelter on the roof of my family's house. I then made cages out of plywood so I could house and breed the chinchillas. My parents visited us in Mexico every six months, so at first they didn't notice my emerging business, but every time they came back I had more and more of these miniature creatures. It got to the point that I had to hire my younger sister, Lupe, to feed them, care for them and clean their cages. When I had 500 chinchillas, I became a member of the Chinchilla Breeders' Association, whose headquarters were in Mexico City. Its job was to collect furs from different breeders and send them to the US, where they were gathered in batches of homogeneous color. The breeders were paid only after the furs were sold in auctions.

I never did get to sell furs; instead, I went to the U.S. and brought back chinchillas in new colors, hybrids resulting from crossing different breeds, since a chinchilla was worth more as a stud than the value of its fur. I bred these new specimens and sold the litters as breeding stock, which was much more profitable. To commercialize them, I leased a property at 1777 Insurgentes Sur Avenue and borrowed the street number to give the business its name: "Diseño 1777". A friend who sold furniture lent me some of his pieces, so I created a business that combined the sale of furniture and chinchillas. That store did not last long, but it gave me the name «Diseño» for my next store in a shopping mall called Plaza Satélite.

One day, one of my regular customers offered to buy all my chinchillas. As the saying goes: «A bird in the hand is worth two in the bush!» Or as they say back home: «*Más vale tianguistengo que tianguistuve.*» So I sold them all. That was my first formal business experience.

For a young man who lived in his parents' house and had no living expenses, my income was substantial. Our parents taught all their children that we had to contribute a portion of our salaries to our family, which in my case was quite a sum, although it was modest considering all domestic expenses. Still, I was able to save enough to buy a VW Beetle like the one my family already had and, some time later, a plot of land where I built my first house.

For me, the underground world is full of mysticism: the prospect of walking, swimming and flying across a world normally inaccessible to us makes me giddy with excitement. A case in point is my first house in the Vista del Valle neighborhood just outside Mexico City, which people called «La Casa de la Cueva», or «The Cave House». The plot of land I built it on was at the top of a hill, so the hill had to be cut to make a road, leaving a steep rock face as the façade and the building site at the very top of the hill. I carved a 65-foot tunnel out of the rock—the first 65 feet from the little more than 98 thousand feet I have dug so far in the parks and sinkholes, the cenotes. At the end of the tunnel was a staircase lit by light that filtered through a 98 by 98-inch stained-glass skylight in the center of a four-sided inclined roof.

I used to go hiking over the hills behind my house where springs flowed. It is a great mystery to me how this water flows from the bowels of the Earth: pure, clean drinking water. These are Nature's miracles.

After ten years together, my first girlfriend, Eva Paulina Morones López, and I decided to get married. We had our wedding ceremony in 1970 at a former convent, the Ex Convento de Tepoztlán, to the sounds of pre-Hispanic instruments, the woodwind chirimías and the teponaxtle drums. My parents-in-law had an orchard at the bottom of the Tepozteco hill, where we held the reception. A few days later, I left my job at Computadoras y Sistemas. This was a turning point in my life: I was giving up living under my parents' roof to get married and start a new family. It was the beginning of the rest of my life and I decided that in order to be happy I could not work for anybody else, that I had to do what I loved, even if at that moment I didn't have the slightest idea of what I was going to do.

«CHOOSE A JOB YOU LOVE, AND YOU WILL NEVER HAVE TO WORK A DAY IN YOUR LIFE».

CONFUCIO

THE 21st CENTURY LAMP

Shortly after I got married, I designed a decorative modernist table lamp made out of ceramic, with a white glass light bulb inside. It looked somewhat like the head of an astronaut wearing a helmet. I would buy each separate part on Victoria street in downtown Mexico City, where all electrical accessories are sold: fittings, the cord with a molded-in plug, and the bulb holder. In my in-laws' dining room, I would screw the lighting swith into the cord. I got the glass sphere and the ceramic piece directly from factories. Eva would glue a felt cover to the base of the lamp to hide the electrical instal- lation and to prevent it from scratching the tabletops. Then, I would go out and offer my lamps to the modern design stores emerging in those days: Space, Logado, and Gurú. I took orders over the phone at my in-laws' house and deliv- ered them myself on the same day.

A year after getting married, my first handsome son, Luis Miguel, was born. David came two years later, «curious-look- ing», as my granny used to say. On that day, I was working on my lamps in the hospital room when my mother-in-law, Doña Elenita, suddenly began helping me; anything to hurry things along and avoid the embarrassment of her son-in- law's mess. My son's birth made me immensely happy, but I had to keep working, even harder after that day.

At the ceramic factory, I noticed they were making other objects, like a slender hand-painted cat. I asked them to sell this and other products to me, unpainted, and started cre- ating my own designs, which I sold along with my lamp. By expanding my sales offer, the wholesale business got more interesting both for me, since my trips became more prof- itable, and for my customers, because they could get more products from the same supplier.

The 21st Century Lamp marks the beginning of my ventures in the furniture, decoration and gift business. It was one of the top five products in the stores, selling tens of thousands of pieces in its lifetime.

MY FIRST STORE AND THE 70s AMAZON

As I visited stores, I got to know their owners and other sup- pliers, and I started making friends in the business. From our chats, I got information about costs, daily sales figures, prof- its, and rent costs for business spaces. I used to ask them whether they would help me out with their merchandise if I opened a store, and their answer was always: «Count on it.»

One year after my marriage, the Plaza Satélite shopping mall opened and I went there with my wife and our new baby. As soon as we arrived, I told Eva: «We must open a store here.» I went to the mall's offices and told them I wanted a retail space. They only had one left: it had a 14-feet wide frontage and was 49-feet deep and was the farthest away from everything, but also closest to the Liverpool department store, which would open soon. I took it and borrowed some money from one of my wife's aunts who had always helped us. When the store opened, it offered a variety of products from my supplier friends. It took some time to pick up, but as soon as Liverpool opened its doors, it took off. That is where the first Diseño store in our chain began, in 1971.

A couple of years later, architect José Pineda Arenas and I became partners. He was the manager and handled all finances quite well, while I was in charge of the products because of my natural inclination towards the bohemian and aesthetic, besides having a keen eye for all things commercial. We expanded at full throttle, opening several stores: one on Salamanca street, in front of Palacio de Hierro department store; another one—the nicest—on Insurgentes Sur Avenue, diagonally across the street from Insurgentes Theater, store we built on a lot with a 10-year lease.

Little by little, I introduced more pieces and developed a very strong line. Our Adam and Eve figures sold a lot: two human silhouettes made of wood, one with an appendage from which hung two small balls attached by a nylon thread; the other, a small opening. Some young buyers even asked for the names pyrographed into the figurines to be replaced by the names of their boyfriends or girlfriends. Another product that was conspicuous in many houses during the 70s was a Danish lamp with hundreds of luminescent fibers, whose tips changed color.

On Christmas, we launched a mail order catalog for phone sales, which we sent by mail or courier service to thousands of homes and business addresses. Gift-wrapped orders were delivered to customers' homes. We were pioneers of this type of sales in Mexico, nearly 50 years ago. At one point, we had about 500 thousand clients in our address book. Picture an Amazon of sorts, when having a phone was a luxury, when only the national postal service, Correos de México, provided courier services. Regardless, brochure, catalog, and phone sales amounted to 12% of our total sales, which was no small feat back then. These were the best stores of their kind at the time.

My sources of inspiration were architecture, design, and nature magazines, such as *Architectural Digest*, *Arredamenti*, *Interior Design* and *National Geographic*. There was no Pinterest. When I liked something, I would mark the place with a bookmark to make it easier to go back to. Later, I felt more emboldened and tore the pages off, stuck them in folders sorted by topic: flowers, ceramic, lamps, chairs, living room sets, tables, fabrics, imports, crockery, glassware, paintings, accessories, baskets, crafts, gifts, decoration, sculptures.

Nowadays, in step with the modern world, I keep an archive of photos in folders on my cell phone and on Pinterest: Cancún's Cathedral, Xcaret's henequen hacienda, Xavage, Xibalbá, Xcaret, Xplor, Xel-Há, stairs, tombs, show, publicity, Mexico, construction, bathrooms, architecture, hotel, swimming pools, gardening, signage, logs, equipment, nature, wisdom, music, health, family, friends, jokes, ideas, Miguel Quintana, agreements, cards, games, food and drinks, stores, restaurants, recreational activities. I use them as my inspiration and archive of files with budgets, documents, information, letters and catalogs. All the time, I am updating, deleting or adding new photos of products and ideas. My cell phone is my computer, I have nothing else.

PARTING WAYS

After being equal partners in the stores for six years, architect Pineda and I had to split our business in half. By family agreement, he and his siblings decided to become independent from their business partners or bosses in whatever business ventures they were involved. One of them started a foundation pile business, another one launched his own magazine, and my partner kept 50% of our stores; we both kept the same name: «Diseño.»

With this operation, my partner became my competitor overnight, and I had to act promptly and strategically. The first thing I did was offer a down-payment to buy the four "Shop" stores, which until then had directly competed against our own. The following day, I sent all our modernist line over there—the bright ceramic, the acrylics, and all the chrome-plated pieces, everything that had fallen out of fashion. I changed the concept of my Diseño stores completely and, consequently, the image: I introduced woodworm-eaten wooden furniture, tree stumps as dining table bases holding thick glass tabletops, macramé, wickerwork, rattan, leather and crystal. It was a natural, totally novel and truly unique line.

Around that time, Mexico was opening its doors to imports, and among the first goods allowed in were baskets and natural fiber products. I imported every single model there was, in every color and shape. I received freight containers full of fine baskets from China and the rest of the world. We *sweated blood* in this new beginning, but we never threw in the towel, and soon we reaped the benefits.

Following this radical change of line in the stores, I told myself: We cannot keep calling them "Diseño", and we immediately changed the name to "Diseño Pali". Within six months, I realized they were stable enough and decided to call them only "Pali". That's how I left my recently acquired Shop stores competing against my former partner, who could not make a quick change because he had kept all wholesale warehouses, which did not allow him much flexibility to change the concept in the short run.

At the time, communicating abroad was done via telex. Our telex address was PALIME—PALI was our name, ME was our country's abbreviation. Orders were sent out at nighttime, especially to the East, until faxes arrived. On my trips to Hong Kong, between 1975 and 1980, I saw businessmen in cafés at the grand hotels taking receivers out of briefcases that contained enough power to make those early cell phones work. Who would have thought that this was the birth of cell phones as we know them? Who could have foreseen they would become what they are today, and smart to boot! I can only say that the cell phone changed my life: it made me many times more efficient; it allowed me to travel and resolve matters long distance; to document and notify others about faults or errors needing immediate correction; to send documents, memos, letters, almost instantly; to communicate with all group members and provide each other feedback in minutes; to search for information I need; to make reservations, purchases, and payments. It serves as my video camera, my jukebox, my alarm clock, my diary, and my personal archive. It is what has allowed me to keep up with efficient and agile pace required these days. *It is truly a godsend.*

We rose quickly by opening new stores. We bought the Aquarama building at the corner of Periférico and Palmas, an Olympic size swimming pool where the Olympic medalist, Damián Pizá, once taught swimming lessons. We made changes and opened a store and I set up my office there.

We even had some unoccupied retail outlets, one of which we handed over to Antonio Onofrietti, a famous tailor who dressed presidents at that time. He paid his rent with lengths of cashmere fabric and tailor-made suits, since then, I was dressing formally. A cake shop and café and an antique jewelry store also opened on the site. We soon opened another store in Perisur mall, taking the largest shop unit after the large department stores; it had 7,580 square feet. These two stores, along with the store on Insurgentes Sur avenue, were the backbone of the iconic Pali furniture boutique stores for more than a decade.

I remember the day my mother—I cannot say now whether she was serious or just joking—asked why I had not sought her permission to use her surname, Pali, for my stores. Thinking on my feet, I looked her in the eyes with a smile on my face and replied: «Just like you, I too have the surname Pali, and besides, you also gave it to me as my middle name, so that's why I gave *my* name to *my* stores. I have twice the reasons to do it.» With the biggest of smiles she replied: «You are absolutely right!»

WINGS TO FLY ON

During the ten years that I owned shops, I also flew a hang-glider or delta wing, a high-adrenaline sport in which you hang suspended from a glider made of an aluminum tube frame with fabric tightened over the wings to create lift. You have to run off a mountain slope or jump off a cliff and into the void, before soaring up into the alleys between the clouds. If you can't get it right the first time, this sport is not for you. You can't use anybody else's sail, nor can you let them borrow yours, because they are handled differently and are very delicate. But you can ask other fellow hang-gliders to check your equipment, in case there's any structural failure you are not aware of, before your take off. Before retiring from this sport, I flew for a couple of years with my two sons, Luis Miguel and David, each flying his own delta wing.

I remember a funny story from the time when my two sons were young and would come to see me flying during weekends. Back then, my hang-gliding partner was a friend called Sealtiel Alatriste, and my father, who did not like me flying, used to say: «Son, don't do it, your partner's surname inspires no confidence.» It was *Ala-triste*, which in English might be translated as «sad wing». He used to drive out in his pick-up truck, loaded with his equipment and carrying his huge German Shepperd, Lobito; I was in my VW van, with my two sons and two large duffel bags containing the hang gliders, whose wing tips would stick out on both ends of my roof. One day, Sealtiel had the grand idea of inviting two girls, his girlfriend and her cousin. That night, back at home, the usual questioning of the boys about the day's events and that day's guests took place over dinner. Eva asked them: «Who did your dad drive with?» To her great surprise and amid my outburst of laughter, the little ones replied: «No, Mom, Dad got stuck with Lobito.» And so it was: the rebellious Sealtiel had taken the perfumed ladies with him in the tight cabin of his pick-up truck, while we got stuck with the smelly dog for two hours each way!

Fellow delta-wing enthusiasts say there are only two types of hang-glider pilots: the ones who have crashed into a tree and the ones who are about to crash into a tree. I had the satisfaction of proving this conventional wisdom wrong: in my 10 years of flying I never once crashed into a tree. What did happen was that while trying to avoid crashing into one, I managed to crash into an enormous cactus. I remember Eva pulling out the prickles with her eyebrow tweezers every night for more than a month. I was like a pin cushion.

#MUSTDO:

One must learn to calculate the risk, test the waters and gradually move ahead.

I know nothing that resembles total freedom more than free flying, hanging from your own wings in the middle of the vastness, in complete silence, closer to God than ever. At such heights, one realizes that we are nothing on this planet, just a drop of water in an immense ocean.

When people ask me what it means to be an entrepreneur, I go back to that moment when one is at the edge of the precipice and has to jump to start gliding, when there is no turning back. I suggest that people begin by jumping off from lower heights and, as they become more confident and experienced, move on to jumping from higher up.

One has to take the risk, but you cannot foolishly jump off a cliff because you will get killed. In my case, my first crash landing made me realize that ten years of flying had been enough. I went back to looking after the two thousand bonsai trees I kept in my garden, to playing tennis. And I began a new decade in sports: this time snow skiing.

Before making an investment, I suggest you ask yourself: «If I lost the money from the business, would I be at risk of losing my house, or of not being able to keep my children in school?» If the answer is yes, stop! You should analyze it further to avoid risking your family's basic income. In contrast, if we're talking about some extra capital, that even if you lost everything, things would not go astray, then test the waters and take a shot! If it does not work, all you lose is the money invested, and you can't fall any lower than the ground. But if it works, you'll make many times the amount you invested and, perhaps quite unexpectedly, a very profitable business for a lifetime. The greatest risk in life is not taking any risks: you will miss 100% of the shots you do not take.

«GROWTH DEMANDS A TEMPORARY SURRENDER OF SECURITY.»

GAIL SHEEHY

Another important point is taking risks as soon as possible. If you're not married, don't have to put food on the table, and don't have to pay the rent, then you can go broke a thousand times and start over. You can always take risks, but the younger you are and the sooner you do it, the more ad vantages you have, because you have less to lose and fewer responsibilities. Plus, it's not about what you lose, it's about what you learn.

#MUSTNOT:

**Risk your family's assets
to embark on a project.**

In the beginning, I risked everything—all or nothing—, because I had nothing and needed nothing. If I went broke, I was young, healthy; I knew I could start over and was certain that my family and I would be well. In contrast, some people would be morally destroyed forever if they went broke.

My father once told me a story about Lola Olmedo, a great art collector, famous for being a patron to Diego Rivera and

Frida Kahlo. She owned much of the land in the Buenavista area of Mexico City, where the railway station was being built. There was a politician who wanted to take her land away by playing dirty, and who told her that he would throw her out «onto the street, stripped naked». One morning, a reporter asked Lola what she thought about that, and she replied: «What's the problem? I come from the streets, and I've had the best times of my life naked.»

I can relate to this story, because I believe that if something goes wrong, there is nothing more to do, but to start over from where you began.

«LEARN TO BEND, SO YOU DON'T BREAK.»

ANONYMOUS

HALF-TIME

At this point of the game, we're at the half-time break, after a 20-year first half as Diseño and Pali shopkeeper, and about to kick off the second half, now wearing the park-maker's hat.

MY EARLIEST MEMORIES ARE OF A LOVELY LIFE

Our entire Hawaiian family welcomed us at the airport in Honolulu. We all got a floral wreath or *lei* from each one of our relatives. As you can see, **we had a whole bunch of relatives!**

Floral garlands for the head, or *haku* leis, have been present in the Quintana family's most important events, both in Hawaii and in Mexico. They remind us all of our roots.

◄ What to me was an innocent game of skills with marbles was considered by the school's head teacher to be gambling, and so it was unfairly banned!

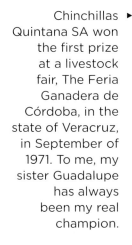

Chinchillas ► Quintana SA won the first prize at a livestock fair, The Feria Ganadera de Córdoba, in the state of Veracruz, in September of 1971. To me, my sister Guadalupe has always been my real champion.

◄ Throughout my teenage years, I built at least 30 crucifixes inside Pisco bottles. The money I got from selling them helped to pay for my personal expenses during that period of my life.

«La Casa de la Cueva» (The Cave House) was my first architectural project and my first experience as a mole. Who would have thought that the 65-foot tunnel I built as the entrance to my house would be only the first few of more than 98 thousand feet that I've dug in the parks and cenotes over the past 30 years?

▲ Starting a business is like flying, you just need to make that first jump.

◄ At the end of the tunnel in the Casa de la Cueva, an antique piece of furniture stood at the foot of a wide stairwell beneath a four-sided roof topped by a beautiful stained glass skylight.

The **21st century lamp** became one of the best-sellers in my stores, and probably all over Mexico. It was my first mass-produced commercial item and my first business success.

These two statuettes, suggestive to some and playful to others, were a best-selling item, and proof that you can break paradigms with the right product, at the right time, in the right place.

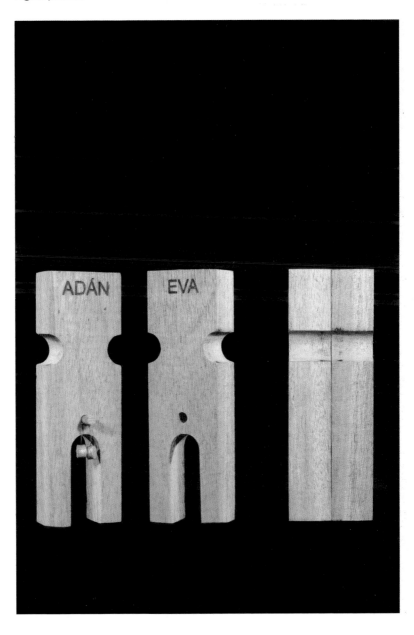

GALERIA
diseño
76/77

◄ This was the cover of our **first sales catalogue**. Just imagine how challenging it was to send it by post to our 500 thousand clients at a time when computers were rudimentary, phones were a luxury, and courier services were not available.

▼ I went around the world, looking for trends in fashion and products for our decoration, design furniture and gift boutiques.

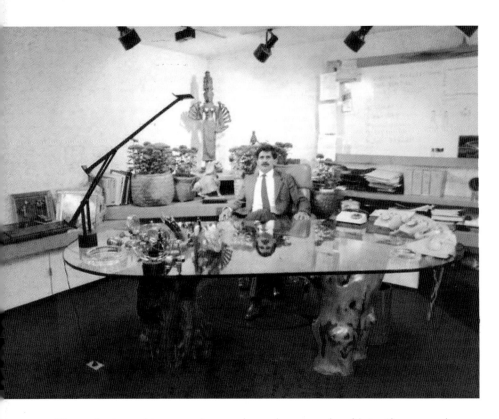

▲ The suits I used to wear in my shops have evolved into the guayaberas I wear nowadays in Xcaret. Still, my desk and I remain the same.

The first store built by Pali, which was diagonally across ▶ the street from Insurgentes Theater, had a triple-height ceiling, allowing us to conserve the trees that were already growing there. This is how I first dabbled in *site-specific architecture*.

colección
79/80 patí

The first store I owned was on Periférico and Paseo de las Palmas. Inside the store was a stained-glass dome, decorated with natural motifs, which now adorns the butterfly pavilion's ceiling in Xcaret.

PARK-MAKER
BY ACCIDENT

CHAPTER 3

In 1985, a friend of mine and a supplier for my Pali stores told me: «Listen, Miguel, I want you to come with me to Cancún. I need to talk to a former classmate of yours from university, Román Rivera Torres. I want to sell some furniture to him. But he does not know *me*, he knows *you*. I want you to come with me and vouch for me.» I did. We met Román at his hotel in Akumal. I had never been in Cancún before. The closest I had been was Cozumel, on my honeymoon, but I had taken a direct flight. They talked business and closed the deal.

Right on the spot, Román offered me some land in exchange for some furniture from my stores. The next day, he took us to see some lots, including a beach in what today is Puerto Aventuras; a cove in Akumal; and finally, Xcaret, where one can go snorkeling and fishing, and where there was a sinkhole—a xenote. He was interested in exchanging land for infrastructure, to increase the value of his property in that area. I was not keen on the idea of having country houses or beach houses, I had never had one. I preferred to go camping or to stay at a hotel, instead of being tied down to a single place. But when I saw Xcaret, I pictured a house next to a xenote, the kind of house all of us architecture students dream of. I was not convinced about the idea of traveling to the same fixed place, but I was taken by the idea of building the loveliest holiday house, the most beautiful one in the world.

I told him I was interested in that piece of land. He was taken aback, since there were only rocks there. I told him it had a mystic feel to it that I could not describe, something I had always liked, that made it a very personal project to me, not for a touristic development, for which a beach might have been better. In any case, if I had chosen Puerto Aventuras, the Xcaret project would have never taken off.

During our negotiations, he asked me how much I was going to invest, and I came up with a big number—fortune favors the bold. «I'll give you one hectare,» he said. But, by looking at the plan, I realized that one hectare or 2.5 acres was nothing, I needed at least twelve acres to build my dream house. Finally, I bought the acreage I wanted and paid him with a batch of furniture pieces he later came to collect at my stores.

When I began clearing the land, I noticed there were water springs, small caverns, a xenote, underground rivers, and Maya ruins as well. Little by little, I discovered new natural features that took my breath away. I reflected and realized that this could not merely be a single house residential project. Instead, I decided to build 10 villas, a change in the contract that Román accepted. Later on, I became aware that so much more could be done with the land: the place's flora, fauna, and past history could be showcased. The project had to be open to the public, it would be wrong and a misuse of the land's unique features to build only houses. And so, the idea of building a park was born.

#MUSTDO:

Fortune visits us all, we must keep our eyes open to catch it. Opportunities are never lost, only caught by another.

On the Hawaiian island of Oahu, there is a place called the Polynesian Cultural Center. It is a living museum of the Pacific Islands and their cultures, owned by Brigham Young University. Students come to the University from various islands across the Pacific, and to support themselves they created this space where they share their customs, food, dance, music, habitat, and roots. They study in the mornings and work in the park in the afternoons as a way of paying their tuition.

I knew from what I had seen in Hawaii that such a project was feasible, so I figured I could replicate the idea, but showcasing Mexico instead. Our country is vastly rich in natural resources and culture: we have many languages, history, music, dances, traditions, national costumes, gastronomy, and a thousand more treasures. I often say that Mexico is 32 countries in one, a world of possibilities, with so much to choose from and move towards; ideas and more ideas. Also, Xcaret happened to be on the site of the ancient Maya port of Polé, and had many architectural structures belonging to a culture that was still alive in the Yucatán peninsula; the place was steeped in history.

I realized that twelve acres was nowhere near enough to build a park. However, Román and his partners—the three

Constandse brothers—had 148 more acres. I reached out to them and began negotiations using the only currency I had: furniture. All was going well, until they asked me what my plans were for the land. «I'm building a park,» I said. «Who in the world builds parks today? Only governments and fools!» they replied.

In those days, Óscar Constandse held the main concession for services offered in Xel-Há, the only park or natural attraction in the area. He managed the larger shops and restaurants at the cove, so straight away he got what I wanted to do. Half-way through our discussion, he said, «Xcaret is the right place to build a park, but why should we give it to Mr. Quintana? We're not selling. We'll do it ourselves.»

That was the beginning of months of verbal sparring, by the end of which I had managed to convince them. I pointed out that the river sources, the xenote, the pre-Hispanic vestiges were all inside my twelve acres; they would be neighbors to a small park and would never grow because my property was the heart of the land. They asked to be partners but I refused, I wanted them to sell to me. Finally, they persuaded me: I believed in them and they believed in me—or rather, they put their trust in a shopkeeper and a barefoot pseudo-architect.

#MUSTDO:

You cannot win every war. Have a clear goal, focus on winning the main battles and be prepared to yield, tactically, on the smaller ones.

After some to-and-fro, we agreed on the percentages and became partners. They provided the remaining 148 acres, and I committed to investing five million US dollars over the following five years—one million per year. This was the only investment made by any of the partners, other than the land; Xcaret's later development was funded entirely with the money generated by the park itself and some small bank loans. It was also established that I would be the sole architect for this project; I would need their sign-off, of course, but we agreed that I would be the one in charge of conceiving and delivering the ideas. I kept my end of the bargain and they kept theirs.

The Constandse family is originally from Tabasco and known for being gregarious. They were pioneers in Cancún's development. Óscar is the eldest, an engineer. He and his wife, Vilma, are the best and most genuine hosts I know. From him, I learned to never stop being amazed. Marcos is also an engineer and, alongside his wife, Inna, a true globe-trotter. He is an excellent manager, passionate about human development. He taught me how to work on a budget to plan better. Carlos, the youngest, is an architect. He and his wife, Noemí, are philanthropists and public relations aces. From them, I learned to be less withdrawn, more sociable, more diplomatic.

Óscar and I hit it off right from the start, because he could see we had very good chances of succeeding together. I had his full support from the beginning of this adventure. His brothers thought I had benefited more from his negotiation of terms with me, and they were very critical of him at first. However, in the long run, they ended up thanking him, once they realized his efforts had solidified our partnership. Later on, Marcos also recognized the project's benefits and future prospects, and became my new protector and ally.

I got the project off the ground, together with Alma Flores Castrejón, the voice and soul of Xcaret's unique character, the connecting link between partners, the harmonious and feminine touch essential to any project needing the sustaining warmth of a family.

In negotiations, you must be clear about what you want to achieve, what your goal is. You cannot win every battle; focus on winning the main ones, and be prepared to yield, tactically, on the smaller ones.

«FIRST, SAY NO; THEN, NEGOCIATE.»

ANONYMOUS

THE MODERN MARCO POLO

My father used to call me «The Modern Marco Polo» because I was a businessman who believed in bartering. I bought houses with cars; I got my first plot of land in Xcaret in exchange for furniture; I was able to pay one million dollars a year, for five years, by means of innumerable commercial trades.

My partners and I agreed that I was going to charge 15% of the total cost of construction to lead the project, the usual percentage paid to an architect. Consequently, for each million dollars I had agreed to invest annually for five years to build the park, $150 thousand would be reimbursed to me as my fees.

At our first building sites, we needed compressors to connect the underground rivers. At first, we would lease them, but after doing some calculations, I realized it was cheaper to buy them. I made a deal with someone who repaired used equipment who promised to deliver it as good as new. With my partners' approval, I bought several compressors to lease them to ourselves. This way, I managed to save money, acquire equipment, and use the rent money to pay for part of my investment.

In those days, a friend and former classmate from the Ibero, architect Oscar Tirado, came to my Pali store on Periférico and Palmas. He had arrived in Cancún much sooner than I had, and had built Villas Sicilia, a residential complex on the hotel strip. He asked me about my fancy car, which was parked outside, took out the plans for his project, and offered to exchange one of his new houses in Cancún for my car, I would only pay the difference.

At first, I refused, but he then suggested I pay that difference with furniture, and I agreed. By the end of that day, I was a pedestrian: I had to call Eva and ask her to come and pick me up. Over the next eight months, he took two more of my cars and I ended up with three houses in Villas Sicilia.

When we started building Xcaret, I would travel from Mexico City to Quintana Roo for three days every other month, then twice a month, then once a week, then alternating a week in Xcaret with another in Mexico City, until I was spending more time on the peninsula than in the capital city. Little by little the park became more important to me. Eventually, I moved to one of the houses to give the project my full attention.

One rule of negotiation says that when someone is buying from you, you call the shots and can ask for more, because the other party wants it. If they are selling, it is because they have a need, and so they have to lower their expectations. If you want to buy, be confident; if you want to sell, do not appear desperate to sell, you must seem indifferent. Fairness, however, is the best negotiating weapon. All deals must be win-win, on an equal footing, balanced and just. And never forget that in any negotiation, as the Mexican saying goes, whoever gets angry loses. The best negotiation should leave all parties happy.

#MUSTDO:

If someone buys, sell; if they sell, buy.

BURNING THE BOATS

From the day I closed the deal with the Constandse brothers, I set a price for the property on Periférico and Palmas
where my store was: three-and-a-half million dollars. Two
years later, when I most needed it, a client appeared, and I
increased my capital. I gave the money to my sister Lupe to
manage it while I was in Xcaret. Every time I asked her to send
me money for the building work, my brother-in-law, Ángel
Gurría—who was well aware of my history—would send me
a message saying: «Don't throw your money away, it's a lifetime's worth of effort.» People knew I was investing it in a
park, and had concluded that I was as mad as a hatter. But I
was determined to follow my intuition.

Beyond my commitment to my new partners, I needed to
figure out where I was going to get the rest of the money
to fulfill my promise. One day, while sitting around at the
table after a meal during one of my trips, I approached Salvador Gómez Linares, an architect and my right-hand in the
stores—he and I used to attend a gift fair in New York every
year, to learn about the trends in decoration and furniture
and to get inspired. «How much are our stores worth?» I
asked him. After a few minutes of mental calculations, he
gave me a figure in millions. «I want to sell them to you», I
said. Taken aback, he asked me where I expected him to get
so much money from, since I was the owner.

«Get it from my stores: start paying me a monthly fee, and
when you've paid me the last *peso*, the stores will be yours.»

An incredulous smile was followed by a hearty handshake. He finished paying me four years later, and that is how Salvador became the owner of the Pali stores.

That day, back in 1991, I burned my boats and stopped receiving an income from the successful furniture and decoration boutiques, which had supported me for 20 years, since my wedding day. From that moment, I started living off my scant savings and a fledgling income from the new Xcaret park. There was no turning back.

SECOND **HALF**

MAKING TRACKS
BY WALKING

CHAPTER 4

Xcaret officially opened in December 1990 with 50 members of staff and a US $10 admission fee. There was a small crafts shop, a museum with models of Maya archaeological zones, a 1640 feet long underground river, two restaurants, a live coral aquarium, an aviary, an orchid and bromeliad greenhouse with species endemic to the area, the beach, an archaeological site, an amphitheater with a capacity of 1,200 people and a cove to go snorkeling.

We showed the visitors native species such as jaguars, pumas, monkeys, deer, crocodiles, turtles, flamingos, parrots, macaws, toucans, and many more wild animals of the region. All of a sudden, we became a hospital and shelter for many wounded, stranded, or helpless animals in the area. This is still happening.

Since the day we opened, a simple fact set us apart from our competitors: bathrooms that were spacious, beautifully designed and impeccably clean. They immediately became a standard to be followed in the area. For me, it was a source of pride to know that even in that regard we had set an example and were being imitated.

As well as being entertaining and fun, Xcaret is an interactive embassy for Mexico's natural, cultural, artistic, and gastronomic riches. It displays our native flora and fauna, our culture, and our roots, drawing attention to many customs and traditions that are in danger of disappearing. What we represent is certainly authentic, but it does not reflect the entirety of Mexican culture—that would take much more land and countless more attractions and performances. Each of our 32 states has its own history, languages and dialects, music and dances, clothes, crafts, food, and ecosystems. Whatever visitors experience, they can rest assured that there is plenty more where it came from, and that whenever they come back, they can find new things.

During the initial development phase of the park, my partners would ask me: «Miguel, what is your vision for the park, how many visitors are you expecting, how much are you charging, where's the profit?» Shortly after Xcaret's opening, armed with the scant data we had—mostly from Óscar's experience with Xel-Há—I told them: «Our goal is to blow people's minds, to be absolutely out of everyone's league. I do not know how long it'll take, but we'll eventually charge US $30 for admission and we'll have a million visitors a year.» Thirty years later, Xcaret charges US $110 for a basic admission ticket, it receives two million visitors a year, and it continues to fulfil the goal of blowing our minds a little more each day.

But what's the use of having tickets sold out if people later complain about not being able to see every attraction, about waiting in long lines to enter a restaurant or to see a show, about not getting a good service? Repeated experiences of good quality service are addictive, that is why we either have to limit the number of visitors or increase our capacity to ensure total xcellence.

Before entering the park, many say: «It's so expensive!» But when they leave, they realize it's a bargain. It's harder for Mexicans than for foreigners because of the differing income levels. To compensate for that, so that our fellow citizens don't miss out on visiting their own «embassy» in Quintana Roo, we offer permanent discounts in all our parks: people from Quintana Roo and Mexican senior citizens have a 50% discount; other nationals from the rest of the country, 10%; children under 5 years of age don't pay, and those between 6 and 12 only pay half the cost of an adult ticket.

A few years back, sometime during the December holidays, we noticed a family happily approaching the ticket office. They all took out their money, counted it, and when they saw they didn't have enough, started walking away. When we saw what was happening, we went out after them and asked them if something was stopping them from entering the park. Mexicans are a proud people and will never own up to having economic difficulties. They made up an excuse, told us something unexpected had come up. We understood the situation perfectly, and offered them complimentary tickets that, we told them, had been left unused by someone else. They accepted them gladly. It was a magical moment. It would be wrong for someone who has traveled from another part of the state, the country, or the world to not be able to enter a Mexican park—especially Xcaret.

Why are we so keen on Mexicans visiting us? Xcaret was created for all audiences, both national tourists and tourists from all over the world, for families and for people of all ages. All are welcome at Xcaret. However, many Mexicans have not had the chance to visit their own country, so we have focused on allowing them to see once more what they may have stopped appreciating. Among the audiences at our shows and attractions, it is our compatriots who enjoy, cheer and tear up the most. Once we observed this, we decided to focus specifically on the national market.

When the 9/11 terrorist attacks on the Twin Towers in the U.S. happened, the world stopped traveling (including myself): the public felt unsafe and preferred to stay at home. However, this made Mexicans, already an important part of our market, travel more within our country, and visit our parks in increasing numbers.

VISITORS

37% MEXICANS   **63%** INTERNATIONAL

#MUSTDO:

**When selecting your target audience,
try to be as inclusive as possible.**

MAGIC COMES FROM WITHIN

Not long ago, a group of families arrived at the park and I got to talking with one of the fathers. He told me the last time he had come was 20 years ago, when he was a public-school student. Every day, many children from public schools are invited to come free of charge, and we offer them an educational tour and a simple packed lunch. He had such nice memories, he promised himself he would return as an adult with his children, so they could enjoy what he experienced as a child. It gave me goosebumps. I also remember a couple who came to Xcaret with their children: one of them named Xcaret, and the other one, Xel-Há, because they fell in love with the parks years ago and decided they would name their children after them. Just think about the impact the xperience of the parks can have on our visitors! This is what we are after: that each visitor has a unique and memorable xperience with us every time, to be able to transform any inconvenience into a happy situation, to touch their most sensitive fibers, and to be welcomed, in their minds and hearts, as one of the best memories of their lives, forever.

The pursuit of these magic moments is at the core of the services we provide. Magic moments must be spontaneous, and to make them happen, empathy and opportunity are necessary. And although magic moments are especially so for those receiving the magic, they are magic as well for those who create them.

One day, while walking around Xcaret with her two children, a woman noticed there was a discarded cookie wrapper on the ground on one of the park's footpaths. Without hesitation, the kids rushed to pick up the trash from the ground and deposited it in the nearest trash can. The family was later wondering why people would throw trash like that. While all this was going on, one of our colleagues was watching the scene. He approached the family with a big smile and thanked them for helping keep our planet clean. To reward their involvement, he gave them free popcorn and sodas, plus he made a special reservation for them to watch the México Espectacular show at our Gran Tlachco theater that evening. They practically glowed with happiness when they received the news! But it was the mother who was most grateful, when she realized this gesture—in response to their good action—reinforced the education she was giving her children, and that this would be something they would never forget.

A few years ago, a newlywed couple came to Xcaret on their honeymoon. During their visit, they decided to try the «Snuba» diving to explore the coral reefs near the park. On the boat back to Xcaret, the husband realized he had dropped his wedding ring in the ocean. Our divers looked tirelessly for the ring for five hours, to no avail. The loss of something so significant and precious for the couple left a bad taste in our mouth. Months went by and—what do you know? —a diver vacationing on the Riviera Maya found the ring! He figured that there would be someone mourning its loss, and decided to share the news of his discovery on social media. The news spread quickly and reached the couple. They sent pictures to the diver, proving they were the rightful owners.

When we heard this news, and with support from the Tourism Board for the Riviera Maya and from a friendly hotel, we arranged for the couple and the diver to meet and share an unforgettable moment. A year and a half after the ring was lost, they all came back to Xcaret. We prepared a Maya wedding vow renewal ceremony for the couple, in which the woman once again placed the ring on her husband's finger. With tears in our eyes and deeply moved, we all celebrated this fortunate event together. The cherry on top was that, after the ceremony, the couple shared the wonderful news that she was pregnant. That was definitely one of the most magical moments we have witnessed.

A few months back, while walking through the park, Don Lupe, the harpist at our Xcaret restaurants, approached me. Somewhat shy and embarrassed, he asked me to help him replace his old harp, which was now the worse for wear.

Although it was not the harp he used at work, I sympathized with him because it was the one he used to practice at home and to play in other personal events outside the park. I do not usually do this—there are many colleagues with their own needs—but I could sense his distress and agreed to lend him the money to buy a new harp. Months later, he came to the office to show off the new harp and to talk about how best to fulfill his moral and financial obligation. Aware of how difficult it had been for him to buy the harp, it occurred to me he could repay me with his greatest wealth: his music. I said to him: «It's nine months until the end of the year. What if on the days I'm here in the office between now and Christmas, when you have a moment, you come and play three songs for me?» Tears ran down his cheeks—mine too. Whenever I'm in the office and he comes by, no matter who I'm with, I stop what I'm doing to enjoy another one of Don Lupe's serenades.

Across our organization, we put the same effort and care into everything we do. I could mention, for example, the initiative by which our colleagues, especially those in direct contact with our guests, wear traditional regional attire as their uniforms—not as a costume, but as an emblem of our roots. At first, people agreed to do it inside the park, because it was a company rule. After work, however, many would usually take off their regional outfits and put on ordinary clothes. They were embarrassed to be seen wearing their traditional attire. Nowadays, the park's uniforms are also their fancy clothes—they wear them to look good in public, and they feel quite proud to wear them. The upshot of these types of actions is that many of our Mexican colleagues have recovered a sense of identity. This encourages us to keep trying to implement similar initiatives to enhance our sense of national pride. I am deeply excited to have achieved this.

STAYING STRAIGHT

One of the challenges we faced when building the park was that, as pioneers, there was no legal framework for us. We requested all the necessary legal permits when we began building Xcaret. Back then, a document «Notice of Proposed Course of Action» (*Aviso de Proposición de Acción*) was required for any project that might have an environmental impact. This document included all the activities one intended to carry through, but for which there was no established legal pathway yet. These were addressed and resolved on a case-by-case basis. We actually never got to this final step, we never got answers, since environmental laws in those days did not apply to the subsoil, or the aquifer, and even wildlife species conservation laws were just being developed. Although authorities were afraid to say yes to us, they couldn't say no. So basically, we kept moving ahead, with no permits, but not illegally. They couldn't stop us, because all our pending applications backed us up. We were in a legal limbo. In this regard, too, we had to break new ground.

It wasn't until Julia Carabias became the head of the Ministry for the Environment and Natural Resources (SEMARNAT) that our status became regularized. She and her team decided to *grab the bull by the horns.* «The development has to go on,» she said. «We will have to impose a relatively small fine, but that will put your affairs in order.» She established the criteria by which any disputes might be settled, and we were granted all pending permissions. Thanks to Xcaret, a new legal framework was created based on the work we have done and on the ways in which we have respected nature: we set a precedent for many regulations for the conservation of wild fauna and flora, and for the conservation of archaeological sites.

We have developed a unique relationship with the National Institute of Anthropology and History (INAH). In the past, many people who found Maya relics in the area would hide or get rid of them; they were terrified of their land being expropriated, since archaeological sites are federal property. At first, we were forbidden from continuing our activities, but we got to the bottom of things and studied the laws. We learned that the area immediately surrounding the site, extending up to 65 feet, cannot be used, but the remaining land, if a privately owned, could be used freely. We signed a 25-year agreement with INAH, committing ourselves to financing the restoration of all archaeological structures on our site, respecting the restricted zones, providing an independent entranceway, and paying a monthly fee. We have just renewed this unique agreement for 10 more years, ahead of time. This was INAH's first ever agreement with a private sector organization. In 1991, after five years of work, we concluded the restoration of the archaeological remains.

We still maintain a close relationship with SEMARNAT. We constantly submit environmental impact studies, both for expansions and for all our new projects. Before granting us any authorization, INAH must undertake a survey to make sure there are no archaeological relics in the area for which the permit is being requested. We work with every institution in an orderly and collaborative manner.

The same goes for fiscal matters. We are one of the main tax contributors in the state of Quintana Roo. Though we have commercial representatives all over the world, we have no assets or capital abroad. Every single one of our colleagues is properly registered with the Tax Administration Service (SAT), the Mexican Social Security Institute (IMSS), and the Mexican Federal Institute for Worker's Housing (INFONAVIT). We do not use payment agencies to manage our payroll. We have a good relationship with authorities, because by now they know who we are, where we stand, and how we do things. Many of them point to us as an example of best practice.

#MUSTBE:

Stay straight, become exemplary

Things must be done properly from the start, no matter how long it takes; we know no other way of doing them. A few years back, getting the right permits in our country was a painful process. What outside observers see in our new projects is only the tip of the iceberg, they may not realize how much more lies hidden beyond the construction work. Filing the paperwork with all the relevant authorities, jumping through endless hoops, can be wearying, although things have improved over the years. Our country faces some challenges, but the point is to keep walking in the same direction, onwards and upwards. If we all do our part, we are bound to succeed.

Nowadays, we have an xcellent in-house legal team in charge of getting all the permits for whatever project we embark on. They adjust our project proposals to make them fully compliant with the requirements set by Mexican laws, and to ensure they are accepted on the first try. Permits may still take months to come through, but they once took years, and are now granted to us more smoothly. Authorities know we deliver full studies, that there is *no monkey business* with us. This is how every project is born, starting off on the right foot. *Saying no to corruption* is part of our organization's philosophy. Our permits keep coming, because we have done everything by the book, following the rules.

«SITE-SPECIFIC ARCHITECTURE»

I call the way we build our parks «*arquitectura al llegue*», which can be described in English as «site-specific architecture». It entails identifying the land's vocation, and making the most of its attributes, while having the least impact on its surroundings. We build what the land allows us and as far as it allows us. Once, when a xenote's ceiling collapsed, a slope with the perfect gradient to make an amphitheater right there was revealed to us. We didn't build it, nature did; all we did was visualize it.

Another example: our underground rivers were once accessible only using diving equipment. So that everyone could swim in them, we expanded the caverns above the waterline, but the rivers followed their own course. We can join two rivers and even make them longer, but it is the landscape that tells us where and how to do it, we work hand in hand. «Site-specific architecture» means conceiving projects that are born from the detailed observation of our surroundings and the characteristics of the land we plan to build on, drawing out its most intimate secrets, its unrealized potential, and those qualities leading to the most auspicious results. Likewise, it entails making as few changes as possible —or appearing to—, sometimes even transforming something artificial into something natural—or appearing to. It is an organic type of architecture, a fusion between landscape architecture and vernacular architecture, merging with the terrain, and making use of the naturally available resources. «Site-specific architecture» is a way of sensitively adapting an idea suggested by the landscape itself, while preserving its essence. In Mexico, to do something «*al llegue*» means to tread softly, or to show caution about even the smallest of risks.

We have also created our own guidelines, such as the «rule of the rod» for designing sinuous footpaths. We trace the

curves by laying down a half inch iron rod; the path's cur-
vature is determined by how far the rod can bend without
cracking or leaving a mark in the rod.

Our unique measuring devices are the «pace-o-meter»—my
long paces are one meter long—and the «eye-o-meter»—a
visual rough estimate. In short, our main rules are to make
the most of the land's vocation; to treasure water; to build
against rusting and hurricanes; to find and harness the new
alternative energy sources; to design and build in a sustainable manner.

«WE MUST OBEY THE FORCES WE WANT TO COMMAND.»

FRANCIS BACON

Most hotels, parks and other tourist developments in the region draw their plans in their offices, some in Mexico, others
in Spain or U.S. They carry out topographical surveys and
take photographs of the land, and make their designs based
on them. First, they clear the land, then they build, and, last-
ly, they make gardens—that is the usual process. We do it the
other way around: we start with our gardens, ready-made by
God and through the passing of time.

Land in the state of Quintana Roo is not very fertile: the
top-soil cover is barely eight inches thick. It took many years
for our trees to grow and we have to take care of them.
When we start work on any plot of land, we make a tree
inventory: we take their photographs and note their characteristics—type, size, value. We try to respect the trees, so
we design around them. In our plans, we try to locate the

buildings in areas where the ancient Maya deforested the land, or in those places where little vegetation has grown. We never take down any trees and, if we really must, we relocate them to somewhere we can make good use of them. It is a crime to throw away hundreds of years of native flora, as if hurricanes were not already bad enough. We grow our buildings like plants.

We also recover the top-soil in the areas where we build, we mix it with the shredded vegetation found on site and with the compost from our restaurants. We have transformed Xcaret and all our other parks into lush gardens, because the top-soil cover is many inches deeper than it originally was.

HURRICANE CULTURE

We must not forget that we are located in Quintana Roo, where hurricanes are not rare; they belong here, this is their home, they have come before, and they will keep coming. With hurricane Wilma, in 2005, we learned that we must plan and adapt our architecture to this «hurricane culture.» Most of our thatched huts or *palapas* were destroyed. However, the hardest part was not replacing them, it was ripping out the foundations of everything that was destroyed, including the posts embedded in concrete, so that we could start rebuilding.

When we rebuilt the park, we used steel in our main structures and reinforced concrete in others, hand-painting them to resemble tree trunks, while maintaining the traditional roof structure using wooden beams and thatch. This way, when the next hurricane comes along, the thatched roof will be blown off, but the main structure will remain standing. It should take fewer than seven days to finish the *palapa*, as opposed to the 3 to 7 months it took us to rebuild the ones destroyed by the last hurricane. Wilma gave us the chance to rebuild bigger, better, more solid, more beautiful. The hurricane helped us wipe the slate clean: it took away all that was unstable and allowed us to build more solidly what was new.

It is only when the park is closed that we can make all the improvements and the radical changes we need. Both our parks, Xcaret and Xel-Há, open 365 days a year, and the only time we have for maintenance is at night. We have made hurricanes part of our organizational culture.

«IN THE MIDDLE OF DIFFICULTY LIES OPPORTUNITY.»

ALBERT EINSTEIN

As in the poem and the song, this park has been «made by walking». It is a park made with our own hands, little by little, anticipating our visitors' main needs and whims. There has never been a master plan. We did not know at first that in Xcaret we would have three underground rivers, a pre-Hispanic Maya ball game, a cemetery, a butterfly pavilion, a theater housing six thousand spectators, and twelve restaurants. Time determined the right moment for every action, for every step taken along the way.

When I first arrived in Quintana Roo, back in 1985, we did not even have landlines. At that time, cell phones were just beginning to be used, and that was what saved us. The first time I brought a cell phone into Xcaret, I took it to the middle of the jungle, to see if it would work there, to make sure that I could, in fact, communicate with others in the middle of nowhere. Sometime later the park got its first phone landlines, but calls from Xcaret to Playa del Carmen were still considered long-distance, despite being barely 4 miles away. In those days, the park was in the middle of the jungle. Today it is within Playa del Carmen's urban sprawl. We had to do a lot of lobbying so that, eventually, calls to Playa del Carmen were considered local.

At present, there is only one more area in Xcaret where we can build a final attraction, but we still cannot envision what we might build there. We have many ideas in our heads, but the one certainty is that soon we will need to increase our capacity, always within the concept of natural parks and showcasing our identity and our essence.

Congruity between what we say and what we do, and our constant search for xcellence, have garnered us many accolades. There are two I am particularly proud of. We received one of them in 2012: The World Tourism Organization (UNWTO) awarded us the prestigious UNWTO Ulysses Prize «for outstanding contributions to innovation and knowledge in tourism», thanks to a business model that blends entertainment and sustainability. We were the first 100% Mexican company to ever win this award. In 2018 we won the Applause Award—considered the «Oscar» of the amusement parks industry—in the category of «best amusement and theme park in the world». The prize is awarded every other year by the International Association of Amusement Parks and Attractions (IAAPA), whose team of experts votes to decide which park stands out as an inspiration to others because of its accomplishments, management, creativity, and future vision.

#ENTREPTIP

Make sure the things you do are one of a kind, and top of the line. Innovation and imagination create opportunities, quality creates demand.

THE
TRAILBLAZER

CHAPTER 5

«THE POSITIVE THINKER SEES THE INVISIBLE, FEELS THE INTANGIBLE AND ACHIEVES THE IMPOSSIBLE.»

WINSTON CHURCHILL

I am the only one in the Quintana Pali family who did not finish a university degree. All my siblings have professional careers. I am the black sheep in the family, although I'm not the only one: there's my aunt, Ana Luisa Peluffo (her full name is Ana Luisa de Jesús Quintana Paz), who was the first actress to appear nude in Mexican films. The aunties and grannies were scandalized, and used to say that she was the black sheep in the family. My uncles and cousins, on the other hand, would declare her to be the only true *white sheep* in the family.

Once, I was applying for a passport and had to indicate my profession on the form. I didn't have any kind of formal qualification, and I didn't know what to write down. My job at the stores was to choose, improve and design products; in the parks, to create beauty, mainly by using «site-specific architecture». Then, it occurred to me to write down «trailblazer», and to my surprise, when I received my passport, this word appeared in the field reserved for profession. Explaining to immigration and customs officers what a *trailblazer* is every time I traveled was embarrassing.

Years later, I keep saying: "That is my profession." In the Merriam-Webster Dictionary, the noun «trailblazer» is defined as a «pioneer», or «a person or group that originates or helps open up a new line of thought or activity or a new method or technical development». I don't come up with ideas spontaneously or immediately. Instead, I connect well established concepts I like to new ones, and that results in original solutions. I have gathered ideas all my life and have made them come true when they mature, when I find them the right space and time.

Ideas lie dormant in my subconscious, lodged in my folders filled with magazine cutouts or in my Pinterest boards. Then, one day, I come across a beautiful piece of land or a new product is needed in the park, and they start coming into my mind once more. I start playing with them, I dream of them awake and asleep, I add to them, take from them, change them, draw them, and develop them through trial and error. I never stop improving, even if I must throw something away and start over. Not all ideas come out well in blueprints, but rest assured that if you can dream it, it can be done. They say creativity is intelligence having fun. The second part, at least, is true for me. *I definitely have fun!*

In 1998, I married Marisol Gallegos Sánchez. Our civil wedding ceremony was the first event ever held at Xcaret's Maya ball game court. We had three children: twins Roberto and Rodrigo and, two years later, María Fernanda, my first and last daughter, the apple of my eye. Nowadays, they all have a professional career, and I am very proud that they want to keep studying and specializing in their respective fields.

Since they were children, Marisol and I decided to enhance their education with trips inside and outside the country. We almost always went to natural, virgin places, like the Amazon, the rapids, lakes, big waterfalls, glaciers, and mountains to go skiing. We traveled to natural reserves for animals in Kenya and Tanzania; to canals in Thailand and Myanmar; to Hawaii, the Philippines and Indonesia; to ancient, historical or almost mystical towns such as Antigua, San Cristóbal de las Casas and Oaxaca, as well as others in China and Japan; to eco-touristic sites in countries like Belize, Costa Rica, New Zealand, and Australia. I do not recall staying at any capital or major city on any of these trips, barring some exceptions—nowadays, all big cities are very much alike, filled with the same famous commercial brand names. No sooner had we landed at an airport than we headed straight out to the countryside, to coexist with nature. After so many trips and so many colors and flavors, I've learned that the most important thing about travelling is to travel in the company of others, to be able to share these xperiences, to travel light, and for no more than 15 days in a row.

«WHAT I LIKE BEST ABOUT CITIES IS WHAT LIES OUTSIDE THEM.»

JOHN GRAVES

We are the result of our xperiences, and I think that an important part of them are our trips. Travel broadens the mind.

These days, when a young person asks me for advice, I reply, «Travel: first, inside your own country; then, travel the world. You'll see wonderful things and learn unexpected ones; you might even learn a language, without realizing it.» That is the best education.

#MUSTDO:

Travel, travel, travel. First, inside your own country; then, travel the world. You will see things you never imagined, you will learn things you didn't know existed.

I also confirmed that the best part of all my trips is when I come back to my home sweet home because, warts and all, *there is no place like Mexico.* A lot of people complain because they imagine there is some ideal country elsewhere, but in truth, it is simply that they have not been able to appreciate what we have. Often, they have had no way of comparing it. And yet it does not take too long for a foreigner to fall in love with our land and our people. Loving Mexico is easy because it offers everything—starting with its warm, hospitable, welcoming, and loving people.

I was born in Boston to an American mother, so I had two paths to becoming a U.S. national, but it never crossed my mind. My greatest pride is to be Mexican. My siblings didn't take up U.S. citizenship either.

Life is full of twists and turns. Not long ago, I needed to renew my visa at the American consulate in Mérida. They gave me two appointments, one week apart. During the first one, after having all my papers reviewed, being fingerprinted and photographed, the officer asked me if I was aware that

I had another appointment seven days later. I replied I was, but didn't know why, since the normal visa process only takes a single visit. He said he didn't know the reason but would advise me to bring bank references and any other document proving my economic solvency. A week later, during my second appointment, the Consul asked where I was born. «Boston, Massachusetts,» I replied. «Your visa has been denied. People born in the U.S. can only enter the country with a U.S. passport,» she explained. After entering and leaving that country as a Mexican for 73 years, and after having relinquished U.S. citizenship at 18, I was now being called that often derogatory nickname for Americans in Mexico—I was being called a «gringo»!

After further discussion I persuaded her to look into her records to confirm that for the past half century my visa had, indeed, been renewed consistently. After half an hour of further inquiries, she said: «In 1960, you relinquished U.S. citizenship in Mexico City. Wait for your visa. It'll be delivered to you within the next 30 days.» She shut the window screen. Everyone else had already gone home. I felt my soul come back into my body. If there is one thing I am certain of, it is that even if I had never been allowed to return to the U.S. I would not change my nationality for any other in the world.

POLÉ, THE MAYA PORT

Xcaret means «small cove» in Maya. It is the name given to the ancient city of Polé by Maya fighters in the Caste Wars of the 19th century who took refuge in Quintana Roo. It had an important secular population, as proven by the remains of its temples and its beautiful wall dating back many centuries. In 1997 we auditioned players of ulama, a ball game played with the hips and an 8-pound natural rubber ball, which at that moment was only played in the northern state of

Sinaloa. It had once been practiced throughout Meso-America but had not been played for over 500 years, so we took it upon ourselves to bring this beautiful game back to life as it was played around 1,400 BC by recreating it in a dirt court inspired by the buildings of Copán and Cobá. We adapted this game, which in Xcaret we call Pok' ta' Pok', to keep this ancient tradition alive and to strengthen our roots by integrating this important Mexican heritage into our park's activities. Today, we are the only place in the country where this ball game is played every day, and we are encouraging the young generations to foster its preservation—a project still in its early stages.

Some five hundred years ago, pilgrims arrived in Polé from all over the Maya world: El Salvador, Belize, Honduras, Guatemala and all the Mexican southeast region. They traveled in dugout canoes from Polé to the island of Cozumel, taking offerings to Ixchel, the goddess of fertility. The channel separating the island from the mainland is 11 miles wide and has a strong northward current. Rowers must set off on a southward course and row at full power to get to the island. If you are not careful, you can easily drift to the north and end up drinking a mojito in the island of Cuba.

No one had ever tested whether these arduous crossings could have actually taken place. Fourteen years ago, we set up the first Sacred Maya Journey—not because we had to, but because it was worth proving to the world that this beautiful tradition was feasible. A crew of six people and another of eight used two dugout canoes and made it across successfully.

At present, 38 canoes with a 10 oarsmen crew set out in May. It takes them one day to leave and another to return. Over the past 14 years, we've had about 4,250 volunteers, including children, young adults, and senior citizens participating in the dances and ceremonies in Xcaret and Cozumel.

We have reached huge audiences: more than 75 thousand people have witnessed the Sacred Maya Journey, a one-of-a-kind project in the country.

We restored this tradition and made it replicable. The Sacred Maya Journey is a model for the conservation and dissemination of an intangible cultural heritage, contributing to the social and cultural aspects of sustainable development and strengthening the identity of the people of Quintana Roo in the process.

SACRED MAYA JOURNEY: XCARET-COZUMEL-XCARET

8 000
PARTICIPANTS

380
CANOERS FROM
13 COUNTRIES
EACH YEAR

38 CANOES

46% OF CANOERS ARE WOMEN

250
ARTISTS

The Sacred Maya Journey touches people and their life stories in many ways. There are exceptional cases, like that of Marco, a blind man who still managed to make the journey, with great effort and a lot of support from his crew mates. By listening to the oars going in and out of the water he was able to follow the rhythm of his crew. He has set a great example and is now a high-performance athlete. These days, he has passed on the torch to his son, Lihu, who just turned 18 and made his first crossing in 2019. Then there is Betty, who moved from Veracruz to Playa del Carmen for six months to train in Cancún, Xcaret, Xel-Há, and Cozumel, so that at the age of 65 she could make the crossing to Cozumel. Or all those parents who have been motivated by their children to undertake the crossing, or the siblings who come back to row every year, not to mention those who have taken part in every single crossing. Or those female canoers who, thanks to their devotion to the goddess Ixchel, became pregnant, some of them after many years of trying.

Every canoe contains ten different life stories—mothers, fathers, grandparents, young and old, blonds and brunettes, rookies and veterans, the ones from before and the ones from now, from different localities, born in different places. All canoers, joined in an ever-growing community, increasingly varied, including people like you and me, who dare to do something xtraordinary, and who in the Sacred Journey have found an xcellent opportunity to surpass themselves.

DEATHLY ATTRACTIONS

Whereas in other countries death is not celebrated, here it is commemorated with a *fiesta*, a time to remember those who have departed. Since part of our mission is to showcase the best of Mexico, we try to create attractions which can be put on display every day. An example of this is the cemetery, opened on November 1, 2004, on the Day of the Dead. It was controversial at first: «Who'll want to see a graveyard in a park?» my partners asked. Naturally, it is a place to mourn, but we take the opportunity to teach about another Mexican tradition. It has been quite a success: people are dying to get into the burial ground. Today, the cemetery is home to the ashes of my parents, a brother, my Hawaiian grandparents, an aunt, and my in-laws. I visit them often.

To build the graves, I recruited a team of Dreamers: creative, talented, winning minds, mostly millennials, part of the new generation that would help to bring a new vision to our business and who have now become part of its success. Each grave builder led his or her own team of workers. They were in charge of developing a design for each grave and making it a reality. I would give them a picture of a tomb from the region that I had liked, and they could tropicalize it, using their imagination and personal taste in doing so. I was, myself, a member of the team of Dreamers. I checked their progress every week, and if there was a tomb I didn't like, I would nominate it to be demolished by my foreman the following week if it hadn't been improved. People had to be on their toes. To my surprise, one day, they nominated one of mine, because they thought it was too childish: it was for someone called Miguelín (a play on the name of the tire brand, Michelin) and it reproduced the front of a truck framed by a rubber tire. That weekend, I visited the building site with my children: 8-year-old María Fernanda and the 10-year-old twins, Rodrigo and Roberto. I asked them which tombs they liked best, and which ones they didn't. Guess what? The three of them loved the Miguelín truck! *And so, as they say, it lived to see another day.*

#MUSTDO:

Be inclusive. Design everything thinking about your clients: children, young people and adults—they are all equally important.

Just as important as the actual tombs are the epitaphs, because they reflect something about the life of the deceased: their character, their way of being, their work, their humor. Most of the epitaphs on our tombs are real, they were «borrowed» from actual cemeteries in the Yucatán peninsula: «Here lies Juan García of whom we now speak: he used a match to check for a gas leak, and leaking it was"; «Lord, may you welcome her with the same joy with which I send her to you»; «Here lies Vicente, who lived a hundred years, and died at twenty»; «Doña Panchita Paniagua lies here for a long season, she died at 90 for no good reason.»

As a child, I remember going to many states in Mexico to xperience the celebration of the Day of the Dead. It saddens me to realize that some of these traditions have waned. We had to recover it, firstly for the locals; secondly, for all Mexicans; and thirdly, for friends from faraway.

After the cemetery's inauguration, we set out to create a Festival of Life and Death, a project seeking to restore the centuries-old tradition of celebrating the Day of the Dead, which was losing ground for various reasons, including the proliferation of Halloween in Mexico. I took this project on with the purpose of fostering and elevating this celebration, which in 2003 had been declared an Intangible Cultural Heritage of Humanity by UNESCO. The project would promote cultural tourism in our country, strengthen our identity, and it gave prominence to Xcaret as an authentic cultural destination. So it was that we created the Festival in Xcaret, underpinned by a pre-Hispanic conception of duality: life and death, light and shadow, day and night. Today, it is recognized as the most important festival of its kind in Mexico's Southeast.

We carried out our first Festival sixteen years ago. In 2005, because of Hurricane Wilma, we had to cancel all the preparatory work and the commitments we had made, both with local communities and with artists. It was fortunate that we did, because it certainly *ruffled our feathers*. This xperience helped us improve by enhancing our programming for the following year, reinforcing our relationship with the communities, and allowing us to re-start on the right foot.

We started inviting communities from a different Mexican state each year to explore different ways of celebrating our dearly deceased across the country. Every year, our wise and generous guests from various indigenous communities give live testimony of their cultural heritage through their commemorations of their faithful departed. Also, we create over a dozen venues, including a space for children and their parents, where we promote family interactions and teach our future Mexican grown-ups to appreciate our culture and to be inclusive.

Speaking of ruffled feathers, I remember that during the Festival week in 2011, when Tabasco was our guest state, Hurricane Rina loomed menacingly. We had to move fast! In one day, we had to dismantle everything we had set up in a week, while keeping calm the more than 300 participants, both artists and community members, who had come to perform. We had even issued an emergency press release to the public through different media when Rina suddenly changed course. No more hurricane! So, we had to move fast once again, and put out another press release, letting the public know that we would welcome those holding tickets for October 30 and 31 on November 1 and 2, as long as the park's capacity was not exceeded. We also talked to all participants to let them know we would be having the Festival after all, but on our new dates. Back to cleaning the park, mounting all the stages and putting up the decorations—in just two days. Oh, the memories!

In 2012, the singer Lila Downs performed at our gala concert to our first full house at the Gran Tlachco theater. Having xperienced the Festival, completely overwhelmed, she told us she had never seen anything like it. Four years later, she came back with her mother, an anthropologist, who was also powerfully impressed.

Within the "Red Nacional de Festivales", a national festival network, ours is one of the few recognized in Quintana Roo, a distinction awarded to us for 15 years of celebration. Nowadays, it has become an event that is sought and enjoyed by more than 53 thousand people every year. With time, we have learned to issue and sell tickets in advance, to monitor the park's capacity and guarantee the best possible xperience.

FESTIVAL OF LIFE AND DEATH

 53 000 AND **420**
SPECTATORS VOLUNTEERS

25
GROUPS
OF ARTISTS
 23
GROUPS OF
CRAFTSPEOPLE
 18
GROUPS OF
TRADITIONAL
COOKS

When we started, most hotels in Cancún and in the Riviera Maya had Halloween parties. That was what tourists saw everywhere. Likewise, schools had celebrations with costumes, witches, and pumpkins. Little by little, through our Festival of Life and Death, we have managed to persuade hotels to put up altars to the dead, and local schools are teaching children the value of our Day of the Dead tradition. The community thinks of this celebration as theirs. This has helped develop a sense of belonging and of feeling rooted, which matters in a place composed mainly of immigrants from all over the country and even from other countries. What is most beautiful about the Festival is that every year we make further progress in the conservation and dissemination of our cultural heritage.

MÉXICO
ESPECTACULAR

CHAPTER 6

AN IDEA NEEDS TO BE CHALLENGED

In Xcaret's early days, back in 1995, one of our greatest successes, as well as sources of disagreement between partners, was our show México Espectacular. There was an underground river running through a xenote whose ceiling started cracking, posing a very high risk, so we had it taken down. When it fell, instead of dwelling on the loss, we were astonished to see how a splendid natural amphitheater had been *created*, including a space with the right inclination for seating. We decided to adapt it and build a stage. Shortly after, one of my collaborators approached us: «I brought a group of artists I would like you to see,» she said. They became the first to use our new stage, and we liked the result. We refined their presentation, and that was our first attempt to launch a Mexican show called

Xcaret de Noche («Xcaret by Night»). Back then, the park closed at 5:00 p.m., but on Tuesdays and Thursdays it would open again an hour later so people could enjoy dinner under a thatched palapa and, afterwards, watch the show at the amphitheater. The number of spectators hovered between 60 and 120, while daily visitors to the park numbered almost one thousand. This way of commercializing the show never took off, and losses were increasing. We had to find a solution as soon as possible.

I proposed staging the show every day, and making it part of the whole visit, by increasing the admission ticket a little to include its cost. For a modest increase, daytime visitors could see and enjoy it. It wasn't about changing our park, but about complementing it. My partners resisted the idea. They even called a meeting with the Board of Directors and the Group's executives to discuss the issue.

One of the partners said: «Mr. Quintana has suggested including the night show in the admission ticket, and I think it's preposterous. We have the most successful park in the country. I just came back from Mexico City. While I was there, a friend asked me to lend him some money, another one told me his company went bankrupt, I became partners with yet another because he wasn't doing well, others even asked me for a job. Things are bad. In the capital, people are going through economic crises, and here we are, standing strong, with a very profitable park: *a natural, daytime park*. Today, Mr. Quintana is proposing that we put this success at risk: he recommends creating *a cultural park that opens at night-time*, which goes against the two foundational pillars of our success. I am not willing to keep losing money, especially at this time, so I categorically oppose this integration.»

Everyone had their say and made comments. Before leaving, I asked them to vote for one of three choices: keeping things as they were, creating one single integrated product, or getting rid of the show altogether. Board members said this decision had to be made by the partners, not by them. Still, I insisted, it would be useful to know how everyone felt about it. Every one of the 16 attendees cast their votes secretly, and these were the results: four voted to keep things the same, two of us voted to integrate the show, and the remaining ten voted to cancel it. Seeing that all was lost, I had an idea. I said: «Bear with me a little longer: the cultural director has requested that we audition a music group on Wednesday two weeks from now, after closing hours.» They took out their agendas and wrote it down. That Wednesday, they were all there promptly.

A day before the appointed date, we had announced the event to all the travel agencies and operators. We had also asked them to program their buses to take their passengers back home a little later than usual. We placed posters all over the park saying people could stay to watch the show and have the full-day xperience—the way I wanted it to be. We succeeded in convincing roughly half the number of that day's visitors, about 600 people. The show started. My partners were furious, feeling they had been ambushed.

At the end of the show, before anyone had time to leave their seats, almost all spectators had a pen and a printed piece of cardboard in their hands. It had three questions, in Spanish on one side, in English on the other:

After today's visit, please rate from 0 to 10 all the activities you took part in, choosing 10 for those you liked best and 0 for those you liked the least.

☐ Aquarium

☐ Aviary

☐ Beach

☐ Underground river

☐ Archaeological site

☐ The show you just watched

☐ Food

How much more would you be willing to pay to watch today's show?

☐ 0 dollars

☐ 5 dollars

☐ 10 dollars

Please include any other comments or suggestions:

_____

_____

_____

_____

_____

Through the loudspeaker, I asked them to answer the questions and added that they could keep the pen—compliments of the house. Audience members left their filled-out surveys inside several baskets. When one of them reached us, Marcos, one of my partners, took a bunch of the surveys, as if preventing us from cheating by our replacing them. «One for you», he'd say when people had given the show a 10. «One for me», when they hadn't. About 80% of the people had rated the show with the highest number, or as the best activity during their visit to the park.

Then, Marcos said: «I saw the results, Miguel. What's your point?» "I want to make a trial integrating the show to the day admission ticket for a month", I replied.

That summer, I was allowed to give it a shot for the time I asked, and to this date it is still on trial. Six months later, we raised the admission price by US $5—the rise in ticket price suggested by most spectators when answering the second question in the survey.

#MUSTNOT:

**Ideas must be sold, not imposed.
You have to be persuasive.**

In the early days of the show in the open forum next to the underground river, one of the most moving performances was *El niño perdido* (The Missing Child). Two trumpets played by mariachis are first heard in the distance, far away from each other, replying in turns, then coming closer until they meet— the moment the «missing child» comes home. I remember a day when I was watching one of the trumpets being played at one end of the stage flanked by a stretch of the underground river, while the other was hidden, answering from on board a small flat-bottomed boat—a *trajinera*—which was coming closer to the stage from the other end of the river's tunnel. Strangely, there was a moment when the trumpet on the *trajinera* did not respond; then, after the next call, the sailing trumpet answered, and so it continued, until the two trumpets met and the «missing child» appeared on stage. A standing ovation followed when the audience noticed the trumpet player, who had just disembarked, kept playing the last part of *El niño perdido* while dripping wet. We realized that, at some point, he had fallen overboard while cruising along the river, but like a true professional, had continued playing the trumpet. He delighted the audience with his music until the last minute, as if nothing had happened. This is the kind of magic that people xperience in Xcaret.

I thought the show might have the greatest impact on foreign visitors. Surprisingly, it was the opposite: we have discovered that we awaken a sense of pride and recognition in national audiences, even though they already know a lot of the music featured in the show. Despite being tired at the end of a busy day, it is we, Mexicans, who applaud the loudest.

To prove it, we have three indicators: the applause-o-meter, the tear-o-meter and the stand-o-meter—when the audience grants us the highest honor with a standing ovation. You would think these expressions of enthusiasm are seen only at the end of the show, but they also happen at the end of each of the many numbers. One such number is the Old Men's Dance, *La danza de los viejitos*, which we included in the show later on. When at the end the dancers remove their old men's masks and reveal their elderly faces, everyone stands and applauds them for at least a couple of minutes.

#ENTREPTIP:

No grand human enterprise has been accomplished with everyone's consent. You must have the courage to make decisions. A single determined man makes a majority.

GRAN TLACHCO

Such was the success of the show during its first seven years that the audience size grew considerably, until there was no room for more spectators in the amphitheater. In 2002, we started building Xcaret's first large scale theater and arena, which would hold as many as six thousand people. It would be called Gran Tlachco, from the Náhuatl words «*tlachtli*», or ball game, and «*co*», or place. It was «the place where the ball game is played». The stage had the shape of the letter «i», replicating the ball game court, and had a pit with lateral slopes and rings serving as goalposts.

The partners thought that the size of the new space was over the top, since we were swapping an open amphitheater holding 1200 people for a covered space that was five times bigger. Yet nowadays, in high season, there are some days when we have to offer two shows, because we receive as many as 10 000 visitors wanting to see it. Today the show is one of the park's main attractions, as well as having the attendance record for any cultural show in Mexico's history. Xcaret's Gran Tlachco is registered in the National System for Cultural Information (SNIC México) and has been recognized in Latin America for its technical and technological innovation.

«NOT PURSUING EXCELLENCE IS SACRILEGE.»

ANONYMOUS

I have always believed in, and often talk about, the importance of having a high-value product, and of constantly reinventing oneself to always be unique within one's chosen field. Our main show in Xcaret is no exception. My philosophy, shared by the creative team of Dreamers, has always been to improve and surpass the quality of what we already have. Regarding the show, this meant not only working on the design of the Gran Tlachco, but also refreshing a show that had been successful for many years and which audiences liked a lot. We had to create a new spectacle for this new venue.

The Dreamers proposed that the first half of the performance should focus on pre-Hispanic Mexico. They surprised me with an impressive entrance of Maya leaders and their retinues to mark the beginning of a Pok' ta' Pok' ball game with a new modality: a ball game played with a ball on fire, based on the Urukua Chanakua from the state of Michoacán. Few people knew this game existed in Mexico, and it thrilled everyone. Adapting it to be played on stage was no easy task, since it involved having live fire on stage. The first half concluded with scenes from the conquest of Mexico and a beautiful metaphor about the origins of the Mexican people.

Once, when I was in Nacajuca, in the state of Tabasco, I saw a small group of drummers in a field. As I heard them play their small hollow wooden drums, making such joyous sounds, I said to myself: «We have to include them in the Tabasco number, but we should have many more drummers, it should sound louder, it should look spectacular.» We put over 40 performers on stage for this number—half of them were colleagues who had day-jobs in the park and joined the show at night.

We also decided to include the «Old Men's Dance» from Michoacán, adapting it so that it could be seen from all angles— unlike the amphitheater, which had the audience on only one side of the stage, the Tlachco is a four-sided arena. As with the Tabasco drummers' number, several of our «Old Men» are in fact mature colleagues who were keen to learn this dance and now, after their day's work, are part of the cast. It seems like they just refuse to stop, they refuse to retire!

The park's Art and Culture Department and the Artistic Department gave us an operative structure that has allowed the show to be put on continuously. Come rain or shine, the show must go on, 365 days a year, non-stop, and this is how it has been for over a quarter of a century—except for the fifty days following hurricanes Emily and Wilma. There have often been power outages in the area, but our show has its own generators for this kind of emergency. Nothing can stop us, except nature.

Furthermore, these two Departments, alongside an xperienced in-house consultant, have succeeded in assembling our very own cast, so they don't have to be hired independently. This way, we have been able to constantly improve our quality and originality and include a greater diversity of styles and genres—from traditional folk to native pre-Hispanic music—giving the park its seal of authenticity.

Most musical and staging ideas have been conceived at our in-house recording studio, which we have been able to use as a test lab. All the show's audio tracks have also been produced here, with the highest quality standards: 500 musical pieces, including the musical arrangement of our park's anthem, the song «México en la piel» (Mexico under the skin) by José Manuel Fernández.

FROM DREAM TO NIGHTMARE

By 2013, we had been presenting basically the same show for over 10 years in a row. Although the audience kept cheering and applauding, the team of Dreamers, restless as usual, came to me with a proposal to completely rethink the show. It would involve some building work, and renovating the theater's infrastructure: cabins, stages, stage machinery, and cutting-edge technology.

For this presentation of the new México Espectacular, the team of Dreamers showed me the models of two set pieces I liked a lot: the miracle of the apparition of the Virgin of

Guadalupe and a scene from the Mexican Revolution. I was so impressed by them that I gave the team carte blanche. I must confess that even though I was invited to the dress rehearsals, I didn't attend any. I was certain that the other scenes would be even better than the ones they had shown me. I wanted to be surprised.

Then came the opening night in December 2013. The show was changed overnight, and visitors, partners, and executives were all present to see the new version. There was great xpectation in the air. When the show began, we were indeed surprised, but not pleasantly: we were glancing at each other, wondering where the joy and the magic from the previous show had gone. We were watching a sad, slow, stilted, historical theater performance. The elation had vanished... The dream had turned into a nightmare.

Without giving it a second thought, that same night I met with the team of Dreamers and asked them to go back to presenting the earlier version of the performance. We were fixing the problem right then. The following morning the Artistic Director was waiting for me in my office, without an appointment. He was frustrated and tired after having lived through this process, and he offered me his resignation. «Absolutely not!», I responded categorically. «We've just invested three years and US $16 million in your PhD. You cannot throw away this huge learning opportunity we've just been given. This is no time to give up. We've learned the hard way from all the mistakes we've made. All this should give us enough clarity to bounce back from our mistakes and finally accomplish what we set out to do. We can't waste this opportunity.» And that is how we began another process, which lasted two more years.

Six years later, I can only say that although *it's been a long and difficult road*, it has indeed been worth it: nowadays, we have a show that continues to exceed our xpectations, a show that is completely unlike the original, both thanks to the uniqueness and beauty of its scenes and its xceptional scenic art, as well as to the overwhelming elation and xcitement that simply make everyone want to dance and sing. It's sublime magic! The lessons learned have made us stronger.

«MÉXICO ESPECTACULAR»

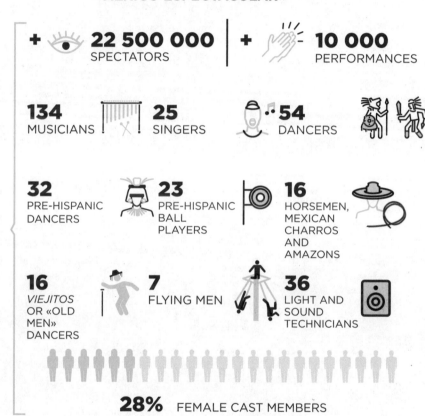

+ **22 500 000** SPECTATORS

+ **10 000** PERFORMANCES

134 MUSICIANS

25 SINGERS

54 DANCERS

32 PRE-HISPANIC DANCERS

23 PRE-HISPANIC BALL PLAYERS

16 HORSEMEN, MEXICAN CHARROS AND AMAZONS

16 VIEJITOS OR «OLD MEN» DANCERS

7 FLYING MEN

36 LIGHT AND SOUND TECHNICIANS

307 ARTISTS IN THE SHOW

28% FEMALE CAST MEMBERS

GRUPO
XCARET

CHAPTER 7

XEL-HÁ

Xel-Há was the first water attraction in Cancún. You could get to it through a very narrow road leading to Tulum. It is a wonderful fish-filled cove, where several underground rivers come together. In fact, it is the final arm of the Sac Actun underwater cave system, the longest known to date. Over millions of years, the land was eroded by water courses that branched out and created this majestic natural aquarium. At first, Xel-Há was operated by a federal trust, Fidecaribe, which in its best moments managed to attract a significant number of visitors.

Xcaret was its competition. Óscar Constandse, the partner with shops and restaurants in Xel-Há, would complain at meetings that we were stealing their customers. There was a simple reason: our products had a *mom* and a *dad*, while the trust had *adoptive parents* and no continuity in time. Both the lack of government care and Xcaret's growth started eating away at Xel-Há's visitor numbers, which dwindled from more than half a million to fewer than 200 thousand a year.

That was the moment when I thought it would be wise to approach the authorities; opportunity was knocking at the door. I traveled to Mexico City to meet with the Tourism Secretary, Mr. Pedro Joaquín Coldwell, who had also been governor of Quintana Roo. I asked to be granted a license to manage Xel-Há cove. He sent a delegation to find out what we were talking about, what our own business was, and what we were doing in Xcaret.

Well into our negotiations, one day he called me and said: «Miguel, I have good news and bad news.»

«Tell me the bad news first», I said.

«Fidecaribe no longer belongs to the federal government; we've decentralized it. Now, it's the state government of Quintana Roo who owns Xel-Há, which means that from now on, you'll have to deal with them. But the good news is...»

«What's the good news?» I asked.

«I already talked to the governor of Quintana Roo when we gave Fidecaribe's concession to them. I told him that I had agreed to give you the concession of Xel-Há, and he concurred with me. So, from now on, you'll have to negotiate all the benefits and commitments with him.»

I did. We negotiated the amount and the license period, which could have legally extended up to 30 years, although he did not want to do that at first. We agreed that it would be for a 15-year period and that before leaving office he would evaluate our performance, to allow for a continuation. I also asked him to present our agreement to the state Congress. The agreement was approved not only by him, but also by the Chamber of Deputies. We signed the concession agreement in 1994. Before leaving office, he honored his commitment by extending our contract 15 more years. Three years later, the next governor in office asked us to review the conditions of the agreement, to which we agreed on one condition: that we sign a new agreement with an extended license. It was settled: we restarted the 30-year period then, and today, we still have until 2033. This has granted us the ease and security to continue extending and improving Xel-Há.

With two super parks, Xcaret and Xel-Há, in our hands by the end of 1994, we decided to invite Oscar Constandse's brother-in-law to join us as director of the latter and gave him a small percentage of stocks. His mission was to manage our new acquisition, rescuing it from the grievous conditions in which it had been delivered to us—completely abandoned and in the red. Our brand-new director was very competitive, and in his efforts to come out on top he focused on competing against Xcaret instead of competing against the rest of the market. To prevent this, we traded his Xel-Há shares for a smaller percentage of the shares but now in both parks. It was all we could do to convince him that our parks—now his parks too—were equally important, and that we should work in synergy, as a team, to make them both the best parks in the area, so they complement each other instead of compete against each other.

In those days, there was an epidemic of lethal yellowing of palm trees in the state of Quintana Roo that killed almost all the palm trees in Xel-Há. The first thing we did was reforest with a new species called Malayan Dwarf coconut palms, which were very resistant to this virus.

The next vital change was to turn Xel-Há into an *all-inclusive park*. In the early days, the admission ticket and the food were sold separately. After, we launched a new product that included the admission ticket, food, flippers, and swimming masks. It was not very popular at first, but after 10 years 92%

of sales came from this package. That is when we decided to make it an *all-inclusive park*: one choice, one price.

Later, we opened a new experience with manaties and the Zip Bike, a cycling zip-line tour through the jungle, designed by us. The cove was already a natural aquarium, so underwater activities like snorkeling, Sea Trek and Snuba were perfect for observing the fish underwater. Little by little, and with the support of a great team, we revived the park. Today we get more than 900 thousand visitors per year.

Xel-Há is a natural wonder. Its majestic cove and lush vegetation are the park's heart and soul. As it is the farthest park from Cancún and Playa del Carmen, most of its collaborators live in a small nearby town called Ciudad Chemuyil. When we started Xel-Há, we adopted this place and promoted its development in tandem with the park's with a strong sense of social responsibility. It made sense, then, that Xel-Há should become the first park to be awarded a sustainability accreditation. At that time, there were no recognized park certifications, so we worked hand-in-hand with EarthCheck, endorsed by the UN World Tourism Organization (UNWTO), to jointly develop a certification model for parks. Thus, Xel-Há became the first park in the world to achieve an officially approved sustainability certification, as fully endorsed by the UNWTO. Today, we are proud to say that it is a model not only for our parks but also for other parks in the world.

WEARING TWO HATS

The first five years were the hardest in the development of today's Grupo Xcaret. Everything was managed by four partners: Oscar was in charge of food and drinks, Carlos of sales and public relations, Marcos of management and finances, and I was in charge of the product. My partners wanted a better balance between profit sharing and reinvestment, a departure from how things were being managed. I wanted more invest-ment so that the parks could grow and be prepared to receive more people. What came first, the chicken or the egg? I was terrified there would come a day when there would be more tourists at our gate than we could accommodate. Fortunately, we have continued to grow, we have improved our facilities and their appearance, increased our capacity, and enhanced our offering with new and better parks.

However, our budgets have never seemed to be enough for us, making any financial planning difficult and causing un-ease among partners. Our «site-specific architecture» is not the traditional kind; calculating how much material or man-power will be needed cannot be done with precision, and this did not help when it was time to plan or set a budget.

There were four partners and each one of us had a vote, regardless of his percentage of shares. A simple majority—my vote plus two more—was needed to get my projects ap-proved. Fortunately, their trust grew with every new project that worked. They were still tough, but the favorable results helped soften and persuade them.

«STRENGTH LIES IN DIFFERENCES, NOT IN SIMILARITIES.»

STEPHEN COVEY

In time, we learned that the only thing we could do right every year was estimate how much money we could set aside for investment. Based on our revenue—which was easier to cal-culate precisely—we established a yearly spending budget. If it turned out to be insufficient, we continued our work the following year with that year's budget. But we taught ourselves to keep within the yearly budget, without overdrawing. This way, we could determine a yearly amount for investment, although not the total amount we would spend on each project, nor its date of completion. We learned to keep to our budget to avoid getting into long discussions among partners at the end of the year. Also, we changed our management structure by introducing a mediator figure, and in 2003 we appointed the Director of Xel-Há as the Group's General Director.

By 2008, this position was already vacant. We hadn't learned our lesson: our former director, who had come from within our own ranks, had turned into our commercial competitor. *That's the way it goes.*

I was already the Group's Product Director, but I was offered a second hat to wear: General Director, in charge of the Group's entire operation, following the directives of the Board of Directors—the partners. I accepted, but I asked for a concession: that I be allowed to present reports to the board every 10 years. A few months ago, I presented my first report about the past decade, which earned my confirmation as General Director for 10 more years.

I took the reins of the company, stepping on the gas on our new projects. I remember someone saying: «Mr. Quintana, you're asking for too much; you're putting a strain on the machinery.» «First, we must take off; then, the dust will settle», I replied. But it never happened. We simply developed a new speed, which people complained about at first, but they later realized that was the new work rhythm for the Group. In truth, it had to do with a new speed in how the market works, and whoever did not follow this new pace would be left behind. *You snooze, you lose* (or far worse).

«THE ONLY WAY TO BE FOLLOWED IS TO RUN FASTER THAN THE OTHERS.»

FRANCIS PICABIA

For me, the change began at the start of the 21st century with the removal of commercial, technological, and cultural barriers; with the world's globalization and with our taking advantage of technology every day in our personal lives. We had to speed up to jump on that moving train, to be up to date, connected, informed. The world is moving at a different speed; your success hinges on how fast you make decisions. Since then, we have continued to grow in an accelerated fashion, always aspiring to be leaders in our field, enhancing the range of touristic entertainment we offer. Fortunately, we have succeeded so far. The challenge is not just to make it to the top, but to stay there. Sometimes, newly created products remain confined because of the size of the site we build them on—the size of a xenote, for instance. But in everything we do we are thinking about the number of people we will be admitting per day for the next 10 years, because increasing our capacity is no easy task, especially in a completed, functioning park.

#MUSTDO:

Take action today for the long run.

XPLOR

In 2005, I came home inspired from a trip to Costa Rica that I did with my partner Marcos and his wife, Inna. I noticed that many eco-tourism parks over there were far more advanced than the ones in Mexico: there were zip-lines, white-water rafting, all-terrain vehicles, and butterflies—hence our own butterfly pavilion. I made the partners a proposal for an adventure park on one of our own plots of land, a pretty rugged terrain that had amazing caverns and underground rivers. They said there was too much competition already: parks with zip-lines, off road vehicles, xenotes, and kayaks. Still, I insisted that our park's success would lie in offering all those activities in a single place and taking them to a whole new level of xcellence.

At that time, safety was not usually a consideration in these types of activities. I proposed creating an xceptional adventure xperience in a completely safe environment, setting an entirely new standard. We would have the longest zip-line in the region with an automatic brake system, amphibious vehicles developed by our creative team, paddling through caves on rafts using your own hands, and swimming in underground rivers. We would create the first underground park on the planet, surrounded by unique natural scenery, in itself quite an xperience. Every activity would be different to any other you could find with our competitors, with the added bonus of all of them being in the same park and included in the same admission ticket. That's how our «*all adventure inclusive*» concept was born.

My partners asked me how much the construction would cost, our usual dilemma. My swift calculations threw out a figure of about four million dollars, five at most, because we already had the land. We agreed to meet in a month to make a decision. When the day came, they said: «We won't give you five million, you'll have 10, on one condition: if the project cost goes over this amount, you'll cover the difference, ours as well as yours.» I was sure I wouldn't exceed this figure, so I accepted.

When we went over the agreed amount, I started covering the difference, until I reached the first five additional million. By then, the partners had realized the extra investment was well worth it, and they cancelled my next pending additional payments—we all continued contributing per our original percentages of stock. It was fortunate they took pity on me, because the park cost was 32 million dollars, not including the cost of the land!

The end of 2008 brought the global economic crisis. In early 2009, it was the H1N1 influenza pandemic. Both events stopped tourists from coming to us. Investments fell, as people everywhere started putting a break on their projects. We were half-way through building work, but decided to swim against the current, taking advantage of the fact that others were holding back. It was time to gain ground, so we ploughed on, expecting to see things going back to normal by the time of our opening. In June 2009, while business closures and failures were being announced all over, we convened a press conference in Mexico City with the news of a new park. Xplor had a great take off, and quickly became one of our most successful parks.

#MUSTDO:

Crises may be terrifying, but they can also present great opportunities. Learn to read them. When everyone falls back, it is your chance to plough on.

UNITED WE STAND, DIVIDED WE FALL

With three parks now managed by the Group, in 2009 we started a new phase: establishing an economy of scale. Under the previous General Director, there was a lot of rivalry between Xcaret and Xel-Há. Each had its own management, its own commercialization strategies, its own policies. When a park representative distributed his brochures, the one from the other park would come along and throw them out; our marketing people would fight among themselves to get an advertising spread at any cost; we paid different prices to the same supplier, and some suppliers would even be bound by exclusivity arrangements in an attempt to stop the other park from getting the same product. There was a frontal war, no synergies, as if they were different companies, owned by different people, competing against each other.

The Group's strategy needed to rely on processes that offered administrative, technological and financial support, seeking economies of scale and synergies in integrated supply chains, all within a legal framework that granted security. The barriers between the different parks, their management and their operations limited the Group's growth and made the unification and standardization of policies, procedures and organizational outlooks difficult. Keeping them separate diminished the Group's growth potential. On the other hand, integrating corporate support areas would allow us to consolidate the financial, technological, legal, human resource, and supply chain processes.

When we opened Xplor, I decided to unify the Group into one corporate entity. I appointed a Corporate Strategy Director who would first work on an integration plan and later lead this team. The first integration directives were necessary not only to generate savings, but also to generate a group perspective in which each area knew the role they had to play in a consolidated organization.

A single commercial direction was created, the administrative areas were merged, and the same happened with the human resources and the rest of the structure. To optimize expenses and be able to start the new park when there was a low influx of tourists, we availed ourselves of the human talent both in Xcaret and Xel-Há—those in positions of the highest authority also became Xplor's executives. It was no simple task. There were plenty of differences of opinion in every respect. We had to smooth things over, manage egos and focus on the future. A huge effort was made in every one of these areas to unify processes and criteria. Integrating the team was very hard work, as was putting everyone in the right place, but once it was done, and with full knowledge of who we were and where we were heading, we moved forward faster.

Thanks to this decision and to the great team that integrates the corporate support areas, we have been able to sustain the growth rate we've had during the last ten years and have laid the foundations for our continued growth. A winning combination: effective colleagues, satisfied customers.

At present, we have very good partnerships, we succeeded in getting all the parks to buy from the same suppliers, which has allowed us to select and preserve the best brands and get the best volume discounts. We normally make commercial payments in 30 or 60 days, but now we also have productive chains that allow our suppliers to go to the bank to collect their payments with the invoices we have signed off on. Also, we began consuming locally, which allowed us to have fresher perishables and to save considerably in freight costs, not to mention the sizeable economic spillover brought about to the local community.

On the commercial side of things, we launched package deals, because with three parks, we could put together a more enticing product with better discounts when buying admission to two or three parks at the same time, something our competitors could not do. With these changes, we became more efficient, thanks to the synergies produced; it all began merging and flowing.

We had another major learning xperience from our previous commercial model of tours to Xcaret and Xel-Há. Before, we had a concession agreement with tour operators who sold packages, offering transportation to the parks from Cancún and the Maya Riviera. Having an intermediary between us and visitors weakened our bargaining position and gave up a large part of our income to a third party. That was precisely why, at the same time Xplor was born, we decided it should have its own transportation fleet to provide the full xperience: from the hotel where tourists are staying to the park and back. This way, we also ensured quality service from beginning to end. At the same time, we took back our bargaining power with our customers and succeeded in boosting Xplor's market penetration. This decision revolutionized our park world and began a process that would make us become *touristers*, as we would provide an integral service for the tourists, from the time they arrive to the time they leave, and we would offer them all the entertainment they required inside our parks.

XICHÉN, TULUM, COBÁ

It has been one of the features of this new Group management that we now carry out surveys for everything: we need to know what people like and what they don't. The things they like inspire us to improve our products; if there are things they don't, we either correct them or we immediately discard them. We almost always got low scores on the transportation from the hotel to the parks and back. This worried us a lot, because our potential perfect score was marred by failing on the outsourced transportation services provided by those who sold our tours. What we want is for customers to enjoy the full xperience, and to make sure that it is the best they can have. In 2010, based on our proven success operating and offering the full tour service to Xplor, we decided the best thing was to introduce our own buses, drivers and tour guides—all given the training that distinguishes us in all our parks. In Cancún, we set up a bus transfer hub and in Xcaret we set up the bus-maintenance garages.

Before, a bus would stop at different hotels and pick up people who were going to a specific park, another bus would pick up others going elsewhere, and so on. They were like milk wagons, stopping everywhere and taking forever. Now, transfers are quite simple: a vehicle arrives at each hotel and picks up all the people going to any of our tours, and drops them off at our central transfer hub— which is next to Cancún's airport—where other buses are waiting to take them at once and directly to each of our different destinations. We no longer make people ride from hotel to hotel, reducing the time our visitors spend traveling on a bus by at least 30 minutes. Thanks to these efficiencies and to the quality and number of vehicles in our bus fleet, we've succeeded in obtaining a perfect 10 score from start to finish.

At the same time, we realized that we could extend the xperience we offered to include other important sites in the region, without limiting ourselves to our own parks. Beyond wanting to compete for tourists' choice of amusement, we wondered whether we might be able to provide them with everything they're looking for, including archaeological sites, while guaranteeing the safe and high-quality xperience that we always offer. Thus, we put our buses to good use and started offering tours to the most emblematic archaeological sites: first, Tulum; then, Chichén Itzá (Xichén); and finally, Cobá—with plans to reach Uxmal soon.

So, with three tours and three parks we could put together packages offering greater variety, which gave us a great boost, commercially speaking. Nowadays, packages represent 22% of our total sales. This strategy allowed us to attract more visitors by diversifying our offer with some of the popular tours (after our own parks).

Rather than trying to convince them not to go to other places, we decided to take them to those very places ourselves by offering the Xcaret Xperience. Anyone can rent a bus and make a tour to Chichén Itzá, it's as simple as that. We, on the other hand, send an INAH-certified guide along with the passengers for every group of 25 people. In fact, in Xcaret we have a school for guides specializing in Maya history, where we offer training to our guides as well as to our competitors', if they so choose. We supplemented the tour with everything else needed to enjoy this trip, like maps, audio-guides, umbrellas, and a reusable thermos with drinking water.

For Tulum and Cobá, we take the tourists to the archaeological sites, afterwards they have lunch and swim in Xel-Há. For the Xichén luxury tour, we acquired an old house in the colonial city of Valladolid, a block away from the downtown center, where we stop on the return journey to eat a delicious Yucatecan buffet, stroll in the center of the city, and visit a xenote. Also, our buses have two bathrooms, one for ladies and another one for gentlemen (ladies always appreciate this).

This way, we have succeeded in attracting half the tours going to Chichén Itzá from Quintana Roo, because we have become a symbol of quality, safety, culture, and entertainment. Like I said, we are now *touristers*, that is, we provide an integral service to the tourists, taking them to the main places to visit in the area and taking them back to their hotels, safe and sound.

GRUPO XCARET TRUST

Because 85% of family businesses disappear by the third generation, all of us partners realized that the parks and their philosophy are far more important than the company itself, and that we should protect this legacy to ensure its continuation over time. Our parks are far above the partners' personal interests and those of our heirs.

That is why in December 2010 we created a trust whose spirit is to maintain the corporate stocks within our families for the next hundred years, by setting the policies and rules of the game for the company's operation, development, and growth. In short: we cannot sell or securitize our shares. We organized our corporate governance and established mandates for future generations. Our successors can only draw profits in a controlled manner, because the income must be allocated as follows: between 13% and 18% to park maintenance and 50% to reinvestment in new developments. In case of a natural disaster, rebuilding is priority, ahead of profit sharing. Also, we have ensured that 100% of the Group's capital is Mexican. The advantage of setting up this trust is that we are bequeathing a well-oiled machine that, all being well, will protect and support our successors in perpetuity.

We've poured more than 20 years of our xperience into this instrument to make sure that Xcaret continues to be the world's window into Mexico and that our parks remain a very important destination for visitors. We have been operating under this umbrella for 10 years and our corporate governance has been streamlined, allowing the businesses to consolidate and diversify without losing sight of our philosophy, our vision and our mission: «Make the planet happier by spreading our great love for Mexico.»

XPLOR FUEGO, *KILLING TWO BIRDS WITH ONE STONE*

In high season, Xplor was at full capacity, completely packed and facing an ever-growing demand. People would travel to the park only to realize that if they got there at mid-morning they could not get in. They didn't even know us and they were already angry at us! Xplor Fuego was born out of this need: to satisfy the very high demand for our daylight product.

We thought of extending the schedule into the night, but we didn't want more of the same thing. Commercially speaking, we knew that we had to position it as a completely different product: to fly through the night-time darkness under a starry sky and suddenly cross through rings of fire; to navigate through our caverns and rivers as if journeying through geysers and lava; and to drive the amphibious vehicles in the jungle night.

We made an effort to create a differentiated product that would also cater to a distinct market niche: family-oriented, yes, but younger, more intrepid. Besides, when it's so hot in the summer, the night's fresher air is ideal for those who cannot stand high temperatures. It is a lot nicer to stand under the moon's light than under the sun's rays. Xplor is our most expensive product, which is a drawback to many people. As the Xplor Fuego route is shorter, we decided to lower its price. This new differentiated product really helped us to address our space limitations, and we also used this opportunity to cater to another market niche. *We killed two birds with one stone* and now we have two parks in one.

There's a funny anecdote from the first day we tested a steam machine in one of the caverns in the amphibious vehicle route. During the test, it began producing a lot of steam. Few people in the park knew how these machines worked.

A member of staff saw billowing «smoke» considered it his responsibility to activate the fire alarm. Five minutes later, we had several park rangers on site, armed with fire extinguishers.

Another memorable occasion was the blaze at the ring of fire in the Jaguar tower, the tallest and longest in the zip-line courses. It was 8 p.m., and ten of us were there, all wearing helmets and harnesses, ready to test the new Xplor Fuego attraction, which entailed flying on a zip-line through a ring of fire. Once you are on the zip-line, there is no turning back. When someone ordered «Start the fire!», we saw the ring burst into huge flames—we had spared no expense on the gas. For 15 or 20 seconds we stood stock-still—that's no exaggeration. No one said: «I'll go first.» After this initial silence, we all laughed together and, of course, very democratically pointed to the maintenance supervisor—the person in charge of the gas installation—as the chosen one. As we geared him up for the launch, we joked: «You really outdid yourself! That was way too much gas, you only need a little.» The test was a success, and we all relaxed.

XENOTES, A LESSON ABOUT COMPETITION

Throughout my life, certain things have marked me. I have always had a great love of caverns, tunnels, and water. Hence my great passion for sink holes or *cenotes* (for us, xenotes), a combination of caverns and underwater rivers, authentic Maya oases. The house I dreamed of building when I bought my first twelve acres in Xcaret had a bedroom with a glass wall looking into a xenote. My dream was to be able to see the fish from my bed, or to see the inside of my house while swimming.

The terrain in the Yucatán peninsula is permeable; when the rain falls, it filters down into the aquifer, keeps carving its course underground as it has done for millions of years, and finally flows into the ocean. That's why, across the Mexican southeast, there are few rivers on the surface—most of them flow underground. Through the years, these rivers have kept widening and creating cavern systems or xenotes, whose surrounding rock structures eventually collapse. That is why some xenotes are closed, and some—if their ceilings have already collapsed—are open. In the state of Quintana Roo, xenotes are no more than 82 to 98 feet in diameter and 22 feet in height—the distance from water to ceiling. In the neighboring state of Yucatán, they can range from 131 to 196 feet in diameter and 59 feet in height.

For the xenotes Tour, we chose four of the most beautiful xenotes in the Riviera Maya. Each was completely different from the others—four very different types of xenotes. We acquired vehicles to take our visitors to the four xenotes, and the equipment for the different activities in each one: snorkeling, kayaking, zip-lining, rappelling and having a picnic. In 2013, we bundled in a single package all the attractions offered separately by our competitors, providing a personalized tour, using a small vehicle, including not just the driver and the guide, but the photographer as well.

When I proposed the idea of a tour of the xenotes, my partners said: «Miguel, this is too small a product for us, it's not worth it.» I replied: «First, it enhances our offering, it's one more product for our packages. Second, it keeps our dozens of competitors with xenotes at bay. That means 400 or 500 fewer people every day for our competitors; that's 400 or 500 people more for us.» They said: «Miguel, don't worry about them, they're small fry.» I replied: «We were also small once. If we become careless, they can grow, and there's more than one place at the top. Besides, we would be catering for a very specific market niche that hasn't been catered for in the region.»

#MUSTNOT:

Do not underestimate your competitors, no matter how small.

We will do everything we can to be on guard against competitors, because in the medium term we want to cater to all the tourist market niches. In the meantime, something we have accomplished is forcing many of them to improve their facilities. This has contributed to improving the Cenotes Route (Ruta de los Cenotes) in Puerto Morelos.

Even though I am part of a team, I am the one who has to make the decisions—there always has to be someone in charge. I am always conducting my own market research, asking people what they liked or didn't like. When I get home, I ask my wife for her opinion on the ideas going through my mind. She almost always replies: «Why bother asking me when you'll end up doing whatever you damn well please?» I smile to myself because she is absolutely right. I am in charge of the Group's philosophy, pricing, commercialization strategies, products, and the overall direction we're headed. I try to make sure that I make the best decisions. By trying to find a consensus of opinion, I try to ensure that I am taking us down the right road. I am, by nature, my own marketing expert.

#MUSTDO:

An entrepreneur must listen to everyone: his own conscience and the people around him. But in the end, it is he who must make the decision.

Many people tell me that asking questions to get opinions on an idea is risky, because someone might steal it. If people want to take an idea from you it is because they think they can do it better. Make sure this doesn't happen by doing it sooner and better than anyone else. I can be an open book, but I am not commercially reckless. It is like a cooking recipe: there is always one secret ingredient or a step no one tells you about.

#MUSTNOT:
You must be open and transparent, but not *reckless*.

Every year, several Ministers of Tourism from different states in the country visit us to see what new products we are cooking. What they like and can copy, they will, because we set good examples in every respect: with our business activity, our kitchen, our staff and their benefits, our social and ecological commitments, the way we respect our fiscal obligations, and our rectitude following any procedure or requesting any permits. We might have flaws, but we see to them as soon as we detect them.

Having competition is an advantage, because it means having a starting point, a comparison point, someone and something to surpass. If you identify your objective, you will know what to improve, but only from your company's own perspective, in your own way, based on your own objectives and values.

People emulate us—and this is a badge of honor—because we are leaving valuable lessons which promote further development and attract more tourists by means of quality products and better services. One of our main contributions is being emulated, not only in Mexico, but in the whole world. We are not actively fishing for compliments, but we do try to earn them.

#MUSTBE:

Being copied is a sign that you are on the right track.

XOXIMILCO

Xoximilco was a concept already present in our projects, ever since the beginnings of Xcaret, but the proper conditions to accomplish this hadn't materialized. The Group had an idea of building a pier in Cancún's lagoon, Laguna de Bojórquez, but this never happened because it is a big lagoon and there are no sheltered canals or waterways for a ride. It was not until January 2013 that this became possible.

In the place where Xoximilco is today, a businessman used to have a park with zip-lines and quad-bikes across the road from his hotel, but it didn't work. That lot was once Cancún's main lime gravel pit—a *sascabera*, named after the *sascab*, the lime gravel typically found in the peninsula and used since pre-Hispanic times to prepare mortar for construction. The sascab dug out from that land had once been used to fill out Cancún's hotel strip. Later, the place became the hotel's dump site.

One day, the owner called me and offered to lease it to us. Our quality standards and our building methods require us to make sound investments whenever we build a park, so it seemed unwise to do so on somebody else's land. He tried to persuade me, even attempting to pique my interest by saying that our former General Director, now our competitor, was interested in leasing the property. That made no difference to us.

He then offered to sell it at US $25 per square yard in exchange for admissions to our parks. This proposal didn't suit me, because he already bought a considerable number of tickets from us each year and I counted on that income for our operational budget. Instead, I proposed that we maintain his average annual purchase of admissions from the previous year and put the income from any additional purchases towards the payment of his lot. In other words, if he usually bought one hundred tickets per year, whenever he sold more than a hundred, the difference would be used to pay our debt. We closed the deal. We bought the lot without ever paying a dime, and he had to double his purchase of tickets to our parks to collect in the shortest time. We paid for the lot with the incremental difference in his purchases, and in half the time planned.

That is how we obtained 140 acres for Xoximilco's canals and lagoons. Most of the land had already been excavated almost down to the water mantle. We obtained a special permit, which didn't take too long—SEMARNAT had not allowed *sascaberas* to excavate below the water mantle into the phreatic zone, but because these were abandoned lots that were being recovered for touristic purposes, they granted us permission to go six feet deeper to dig our canals. On the islands we created, we planted different species of plants and trees, and today they are full of native vegetation. Everything is green and lush, even though our park operates at night.

Our purpose is to pay tribute to the canals of Xochimilco in Mexico City while offering a different xperience. We have been told that we are competing with the original concept, but we are not. We asked the authorities and the people of Xochimilco for their permission. We presented the project to the owners of the flat-bottomed boats, *trajineras*, and we even helped them improve theirs. In contrast to the quay in Xochimilco, where only day-time rides are offered and music and food are paid separately, Xoximilco is a night-time ride on a *trajinera*, including dinner and drinks on board, music, and a party atmosphere. It is a floating *fiesta*. Each *trajinera* has its own host, and they all enjoy the live music played by different ensembles aboard other *trajineras*.

To personalize the xperience, the boat has a maximum capacity of 20 people, which poses an operational challenge. To have a more balanced, harmonious atmosphere on the *trajinera*, we put families with children together, young people with each other, and adults with their likes. Countries of origin also matter: Latinos are good at lightening the mood when mixed with more serious nationalities like Germans or Americans. Curiously enough, Mexicans tend to assume the role of hosts, they become ambassadors for their country and explain to foreigners all about the food and the jokes. They are our customers, but they are also our partners in providing an authentically Mexican xperience.

Local residents are a key target. On Fridays and Saturdays, Xoximilco goes native as people from the state of Quintana Roo take advantage of the very attractive 50% discount in any of our parks to celebrate birthdays and bachelor or bachelorette parties, or to enjoy our very popular social TGIF gatherings. All they have to do is show proof of residence in Quintana Roo or Valladolid with their voter ID. All other Mexicans get 10% discount, and children pay half-price. The package for the ride, dinner, drinks, and the party is cheaper than going to any restaurant and paying for everything separately. This was conceived as an incentive for the locals so they could accompany their visitors, acting as hosts, but now it is also working out for them as a way of enjoying their family events. Here is another niche in the market being covered.

All our parks have operated in the black since the beginning, except for Xoximilco, which took almost a year to reach its break-even point. Maybe we had the hardest time getting this product started because it wasn't entirely finished when it opened. With our latest park, Xavage, and the newly inaugurated quay, with all the lit up *trajineras* fully visible all the way to the highway, we closed this cycle. Xoximilco is finally completed, six years after its opening.

XENSES, WHERE THE EYES CAN HEAR AND THE EARS CAN SEE

Surveys always told us that 60% of the visitors wanted a full-day tour or park visit, while the remaining 40% preferred one that lasted half a day. Up to that moment, no one was paying attention to this small niche, not even us. Cutting down on the length of a visit was also an option if we wanted to offer a cheaper product, which tourists could combine with other activities they might be planning. Also, we could improve our capacity by selling it twice, that is, offering two sessions per day. In the summer of 2016, we opened Xenses, with the new half-day park model, in a 61-acre piece of land neighboring Xcaret.

For our parks, we have always looked for unique products, but Xenses was truly unique. To my knowledge, no other park in the world offers a similar concept to this one: playing with your perception, your senses, your mind.

The idea for Xenses came from a handful of childhood concerns. I remember a remarkable xperience I once had in Mexico City, in a place next to the Sabatina church, neighbor to the Bosque de Chapultepec park: I was made to lie down, blindfolded, feeling the caress of feathers, and smelling the scent of various fruits and flowers—an unforgettable memory. This may explain, in part, the origin of Xenses.

Personally, this product makes me smile because we are breaking paradigms. For example, we have a river filled with salt water where you cannot sink, and another one filled with mud from our xpa from where you come out more beautiful than when you went in. What lets your imagination run wild the most is the Xensatorium: journeying through different ecosystems in total darkness, seeing nothing, feeling around for the plants on both flanks of the path you are imagining as you walk along it. So many thoughts go through your mind. I always ask: «When was the last time you did something for the first time?» This will surely be one of those times, and for more than one thing.

Right here in Xenses, we developed a zip-line hanging from a very particular pipe, whose trajectory is similar to that of a roller coaster: it goes up, and down, and around. Instead of traveling sitting down, hanging from a zip-line, we emulate a bird's flying position, to make you fly face down, with your arms outstretched as if they were a bird's wings. It was a success. Our visitors loved it, although it also got bad reviews for being too short a ride. We never have the same products in different parks, because we want them to complement— not compete against—each other. This time, however, there was a chance to improve in Xavage the most successful ride we had in Xenses. We increased the height and length of the ride, and thus the duration of this bird's flight. We broke our own rule, all in the name of the continuous improvement of our quality and service.

Nowadays, Xenses is a favorite for tourists staying in Playa del Carmen. The strategic combination of price and half-day enjoyment has allowed 70% of our customers to arrive directly through our own digital channels and ticket booths—that is, without commercial intermediaries, which in turn enables us to get a better average profit per ticket sold. We also achieved another important feat: Xenses is the park with the fewest colleagues in charge of its operation, and not by accident. We planned it this way when choosing its attractions, both because they are interesting, and because they required fewer operators. The lower the cost, the higher the profit.

BATTING
AVERAGE

CHAPTER 8

It would be misleading to tell our story without remembering that we were not always this big, or this strong. During our journey, we have constantly been correcting the course, trimming the sails, so to speak, as there is always room for improvement. Today, I can say that xperience over time improves your *batting average*, as does intuition.

EXTRA, EXTRA

In 1995, I took part in the creation of Cancún's newspaper *La Crónica*, founded by the city's chronicler, Fernando Martí, along with several local partners. I became a partner because I wanted to help this private newspaper, which kept itself at arm's length from the world of old-fashioned local journalism and was therefore free from external influences and political inclinations.

As a newspaper proprietor, I felt it was our duty to publish any news about things happening in the state, without exception. One day, the newspaper started publishing news about the private affairs of the state governor, which later led to severe criticisms of this government official. There was some back-and-forth in the media, the governor tried unsuccessfully to talk to our director before finally deciding to «neutralize» him by persuading many of the partners to sell him their shares. He quickly bought 51% of the newspaper. He fired Fernando Martí and took control of the newspaper the following day. In those days, we also printed the *Miami Herald*, which was of no interest to the governor, so he proposed to exchange it for my shares in *La Crónica*. I agreed on one condition: that they continue printing this American newspaper for a year, without charging me for the operational cost. I would only pay for paper and ink, until I had my own printing press and where to house it. And that is what we did.

We used this same new building to establish Pixel Press in 1997, a sheetfed offset printing press publishing all our menus, brochures, posters, the *Viva México* magazine, books, and the *MAP-A*, an informative guide handed out to all passengers arriving at Cancún's airport.

Once in possession of my own rotary press printing the Miami Herald and later the USA Today, I soon launched a local newspaper, *La Voz del Caribe*. Months later, Mexico City's *Reforma* newspaper approached us because they were keen on the idea of printing local editions, and they wanted us as their representatives in the state of Quintana Roo. In the end, we included a supplement from *Reforma* newspaper inside *La Voz*.

Unfortunately, although a newspapers' main goal is to tell the truth, most depend economically on government resources such as paper, which in those days was supplied by a state-controlled corporation. If you didn't toe the line, they could stop delivering it at any moment. Because we did not accept bribes from anyone, we always had losses and operated under a lot of economic and political pressure. We learned that when you are in the business of journalism, journalism should be your only business. To do otherwise is to put your other enterprises at risk. Xcaret was already an important local business, and we did not want to put it at risk. We used the economic slump caused by Hurricane Wilma in 2005 as a pretext to close *La Voz del Caribe*. On December 2019, we closed the USA Today.

Recently, Pixel Press and Grupo Regio—the two most important printing companies in the Yucatán peninsula— merged with the sole purpose of having their teams work together to offer new products, better quality services, better delivery times, and competitive prices. These are the sorts of synergies that allow companies to grow.

GARRAFÓN PARK

In 1999, we obtained the concession to operate Garrafón Natural Reef Park on Isla Mujeres. We built new, bigger facilities, including a walkway along the coast to the south end of the island, where Mexico gets the first rays of the rising sun. We also built a quay for arriving visitors and an intricate buoy system to protect the coral reef from all swimmers in the sea.

However, after seven years of highs and lows we had not succeeded in making it self-sufficient, so we decided to sell it in installments to our competition. It took them 11 years to pay us—just imagine! I think it was a wrong decision. We should have held on. We lost one step on the scale, and they gained one. We helped our competition grow overnight.

#MUSTNOT:

Never sell to your competition if you are competing in the same market.

SCENIC TOWERS

In 1999, I went to a fair in Seville, Spain. The main attraction was a 229-feet-tall rotating tower, from which you could enjoy a panoramic view of the whole city. When I saw the long queues of people waiting to get on, I told myself we should have one in Xcaret. I got in touch with the manufacturer, and went shopping in Bremen, Germany. I personally negotiated a deal to buy four towers for the price of three. Each could hold 72 people at a time, and they would stand 32 feet taller than the one in Seville. I had to get a US $7 million credit line from the bank.

Two years later, I was installing the towers in Isla Mujeres, Cancún and Xcaret. I bought a lot of land for the one I had planned for Cozumel, but a year after installing it FONATUR told me it didn't qualify as a «building». Since the land had been sold to me for the purpose of erecting a construction, they took the land back and demanded I dismantle the tower. I did put the other towers to work at an attractive price to the public, but only a small percentage of visitors to Xcaret and Garrafón parks would pay to get on. That was deeply disappointing, not because of the money, but because these reluctant tourists were missing out on a unique, xpectacular view.

Despite the debt, which took me 18 years to pay, I decided to donate them to the Group, and add them to the attractions included in the visit to the parks. As an independent business, the towers were a failure, but as one of the parks' attractions, a success. At least half the visitors in Xcaret get on the tower every day, and a good number of them do so in Cancún. This was the worst deal I ever made in my life, but despite all that was lost, at least I learned a lesson: not all that glitters is gold.

CANCÚN THEATER

A year later, at the turn of the millennium, the Cancún Theater opened its doors on January 1st, 2000. The 865-seat theater, located in *El Embarcadero* cultural space, at the 4-kilometer marker on the hotel strip, was the first and only theater in the city. Our first intention was to present two alternating touristic shows every night: *Voces y danzas de México* (Voices and Dances of Mexico) and *Tradiciones del Caribe* (Caribbean Traditions). Although both shows were very beautiful and well put together, I concluded that visitors to the area had not come to shut themselves up in a traditional theater. Two years later, these shows were cancelled, and we started featuring guest theater productions from all over the country. Since then, we have hosted 510 plays, and 1048 school events, courses, and conventions. This theater has been one of the most important contributions we have made to the community in Cancún.

SUMIDERO CANYON

The story begins with the state of Chiapas' Minister of Tourism inviting Grupo Xcaret to develop a park inside the Sumidero Canyon. The partners paid a visit, but we decided it was not the best moment for us to participate as a Group, as it would divert the financial, human, and technical resources that were needed for our other developing projects.

Because of this, Marcos Constandse Redko "Marcusi", an architect and my partner Marcos' son, undertook the project and invited his family to be a part of it. Since they did not have the financial resources to do this on their own, he organized a group of investment partners, including about 20 of the main businessmen in Chiapas. The Constandse family kept only 12% of this new company's shares.

They bought 1235 acres: the only part of land in the area where a development was possible. But the construction work was particularly complicated, because this piece of land is inside the Sumidero Canyon and cannot be accessed by car; it can only be reached by boat through the river. The first challenge was to build barges to transport the workers and the building materials from the town of Chiapa de Corzo and the nearby Chicoasén Dam. Likewise, some basic infrastructure had to be built: they had to build a settlement for workers and a waste water treatment plant, and had to deliver electrical energy.

At the time, the Sumidero Canyon received about 600 thousand visitors a year. Tours were operated by four cooperative societies from piers in Chiapa de Corzo. It was an important market, and the park would be the only attraction inside a nature reserve. In 2003, this new park opened its doors. Though they succeeded in establishing interesting synergies with the cooperative societies, not all of them were too keen on supporting the project.

After it opened, Marcusi realized he couldn't be involved in the park's daily operations. His group's Director suggested getting Grupo Xcaret to operate the park, paying it a retainer fee for this service. At first, this was successful, but the relationship between our Director and the cooperative societies turned sour, which resulted in the loss of their support over time. They united and blocked the ticket sales to the park.

Although it is true that, by then, the company had its own pier in Chiapa de Corzo and its own high-quality vessels, we were taking only 10% of the visitors, with the remaining 90% controlled by these groups. The solution was to buy out the four cooperative societies, with the aim of controlling the flow of visitors and offering a single product. However, this led to what I consider one of the greatest failures in this adventure: the business' corporate governance structure.

As I said earlier, all major businessmen in Chiapas had been invited to participate in the project, leading to the creation of the Fondo Chiapas. But the shares in this investment fund were split among many people from many different industries, with very diverse and distinct perspectives. This division prevented them from reaching any consensus when it became necessary to inject new resources to buy out the cooperative societies and to finish putting the business model together. The partners did not want to make this purchase, and it all went downhill from there, with the cooperatives relentlessly blocking them, to the point of rendering the project inviable.

Six years after its opening, the park's management was handed back to Fondo Chiapas' local partners. In 2013, a decade after its opening, the park was closed. Even today, its assets are still being sold. The canyon became a swamp!

#MUSTNOT:

Never relinquish control or split a shareholder majority among so many partners that it prevents you from making decisions and timely investments.

MUCHA LECHE

In 2004, we were travelling along the Milky Way. I started a socially-oriented company called «Mucha Leche» (Much Milk). We developed a powdered milk formula with a very high nutritional value. At that time, it competed in price and content against the one sold by CONASUPO, the government-owned shops. Our milk had more protein than any other available alternative, plus it offered xcellent flavors (natural, strawberry, and xocolate). We also sold a cookie for school breakfasts, equivalent to drinking a glass of milk. Even though I'm *not* a milk person, I used to wolf them down.

We gathered a team of salesmen and women who drove around on small trucks painted like cows that mooed through speakers on the roof. We recruited both female and male team leaders, to whom we delivered boxes containing 48 bags each at MX $5 per bag, so they could sell it at MX $7 to the people in the community, keeping MX $2 as commission payment. We sold in many low-income neighborhoods in Cancún and in many towns, as far as of Carrillo Puerto, in the southern part of the state.

It all seemed to be going well and the product was a hit, but over time we found that whenever we resupplied and wanted to collect the income from the sales, many members of our sales team had already spent the money—both their part and ours—and so almost never paid us. We could have stopped supplying them with milk, but we did not have the heart. We managed to replace a few of the remiss salesmen and women with others who did pay, but after four years and many changes in sales policies, we could not set the company straight. We had tried to milk it, but the cow dried up.

Some people think kindness is giving money to the needy; but that is a mere palliative to justify themselves. Our goal is to do substantive things, and to see them through:

changing and improving our way of doing things to allow vulnerable people to attain economic independence. «*Don't give a man a fish, teach him how to fish instead*», goes the saying. I would add: help him to buy a boat, teach him how to fish, and then to commercialize his catch. These virtuous circles help us transcend our circumstances. Not everything is about money, we must learn to share, and there are many different ways of doing it: through economic security, education, health, and entertainment, among others.

#MUSTDO:

Always include an exit clause whenever you seal a deal or sign a contract

All these disparate business situations taught me one important lesson: I have always assumed that we are all as good as our word, but it is also true that in life there are always changes and unforeseen circumstances—political, economic, social, personal. You should always put down in writing the financial cost or the consequences of wanting to change what was decided, of wanting to turn back, while still fulfilling the conditions or accepting the penalties agreed at the outset.

No matter how confident we are about the success of our projects, an exit clause is never superfluous. It will give you great peace of mind and will be a form of insurance against misfortunes or changing plans.

GRUPO XCARET IS A MIRACLE MADE POSSIBLE BY MANY HUMAN BEINGS

My partners and I, 35 years after our first hearty handshake.

1985, Xcaret Ranch.

2019, Xcaret Park.

▲ **The Sacred Maya Journey** restores an ancestral pilgrimage done in dugout canoes, from Polé—now Xcaret—to the island of Cozumel, to take offerings to the goddess Ixchel. Today, nearly 500 years later, it is done once a year from Xcaret.

Xcaret is the only place in the world where the ▶
ball game played using the hips is performed every day.

«The Bridge to Paradise», the Mexican Cemetery at Xcaret, has 365 tombs, 7 levels, and 52 steps, paying homage to the way we Mexicans view death. **Ours are the only tombs with an ocean view!**

▲ *LORD, MAY YOU WELCOME HER WITH THE SAME JOY WITH WHICH I SEND HER TO YOU.*

EN RECUERDO DE
Amador Nah Mas
* 04 11 24
♠ 10 02 96

*Querida María,
mil años despúes de muerto
y de bichitos comido,
letreros tendrán mis huesos
diciendo que te he querido.*

IN MEMORY OF AMADOR NAH MAS
11 04 24
02 10 96
DEAR MARÍA, A THOUSAND YEARS AFTER I DIED, AND THE CREEPY CRAWLIES HAVE EATEN ME, THESE BONES OF MINE WILL ABIDE, TELLING HOW OUR LOVE WAS MEANT TO BE.

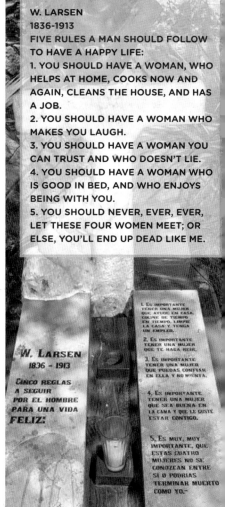

W. LARSEN
1836-1913
FIVE RULES A MAN SHOULD FOLLOW TO HAVE A HAPPY LIFE:
1. YOU SHOULD HAVE A WOMAN, WHO HELPS AT HOME, COOKS NOW AND AGAIN, CLEANS THE HOUSE, AND HAS A JOB.
2. YOU SHOULD HAVE A WOMAN WHO MAKES YOU LAUGH.
3. YOU SHOULD HAVE A WOMAN YOU CAN TRUST AND WHO DOESN'T LIE.
4. YOU SHOULD HAVE A WOMAN WHO IS GOOD IN BED, AND WHO ENJOYS BEING WITH YOU.
5. YOU SHOULD NEVER, EVER, EVER, LET THESE FOUR WOMEN MEET; OR ELSE, YOU'LL END UP DEAD LIKE ME.

W. LARSEN
1836 - 1913
CINCO REGLAS
A SEGUIR
POR EL HOMBRE
PARA UNA VIDA
FELIZ:

1. ES IMPORTANTE TENER UNA MUJER QUE AYUDE EN CASA, COCINE DE TIEMPO EN TIEMPO, LIMPIE LA CASA Y TENGA UN EMPLEO.

2. ES IMPORTANTE TENER UNA MUJER QUE TE HAGA REÍR.

3. ES IMPORTANTE TENER UNA MUJER QUE PUEDAS CONFIAR EN ELLA Y NO MIENTA.

4. ES IMPORTANTE TENER UNA MUJER QUE SEA BUENA EN LA CAMA Y QUE LE GUSTE ESTAR CONTIGO.

5. ES MUY, MUY IMPORTANTE, QUE ESTAS CUATRO MUJERES NO SE CONOZCAN ENTRE SÍ O PODRÍAS TERMINAR MUERTO COMO YO.

◀ Every night, over 300 artists perform our best folk music and dances on stage for 6 thousand spectators at the Gran Tlachco theater in Xcaret, so that all visitors can feel Mexico in their hearts and under their skin: **«México en la piel»**.

▼ God's hand is upon this place. Xel-Há is the most beautiful natural aquarium in Mexico.

Xplor is an adventure in the bowels of the earth, with millenary stalactites and stalagmites as the backdrop.

Xenotes, a Maya oasis, a source of life and spiritual haven for our ancestors in the Yucatán península.

The **Xenses** town is a fun place that defies logic and breaks all paradigms. Here, nothing is what it seems.

Xoximilco, Cancún, a homage to Xochimilco in Mexico City, a very Mexican floating fiesta.

WHEN YOU GO TO XCARET,
DON'T FORGET TO VISIT CANCÚN

CHAPTER 9

Our Commercial Director joined the company in 2004, and in 2010 I asked her to be part of the new team of executives as head of marketing, advertising, and sales, which alongside the areas related to product and human talent, are probably the most important in the Group. Together, we redirected our strategies and implemented new policies and campaigns to get an edge over the competition, to get more people into our parks, and to keep our competitors at bay. To do this, we applied the latest trends in marketing and digital technologies.

Since 2017 our strategies and actions have taken on a global perspective, not only dealing with the parks and tours, but accommodating our hotels as well. Whether it is about managing the marketing, implementing digital strategies, advertising in the countries of origin, or commercializing weddings, we manage it all at Group level, with a commercially unified team, always mindful of each brand's identifying features and strategies.

EGGS IN DIFFERENT BASKETS

Marketing is vital, as we need to persuade two parties: the agents or intermediaries to whom we are selling, and the actual customers. Travel agencies based in the area are one of our greatest commercial allies. They have joined us on our journey and have supported our parks over all these years. We work with online and offline travel agencies in all major cities in Mexico and the U.S. This was an important step in our original strategy, because traditionally, these agencies only offered their clients the airplane-and-hotel package, whereas now they also recommend all the activities available at their customers' final destination and can earn a sales commission.

However, this has not been an easy road, because many agencies demand huge commissions—clearly the driver behind their salesmanship—from those of us who provide tours and excursions in Cancún and the Riviera Maya. If you want to go into this market and you want an agency to promote you, you most likely will have to pay a 50% to 60% sales commission on the final price of your product. We have never been comfortable with this situation, so our commercial strategy, which aims to balance the usual sales channels with more direct sales, has become increasingly important.

In fact, the highest commissions that travel agencies earn do not come from the unit sales of our products. Still, we have succeeded in positioning them as aspirational products, by developing a solid marketing strategy that places us as leaders. Today, half of the tours taken to our destinations are sold directly by Grupo Xcaret, and 25% of our customers are repeat visitors. This is because our parks are permanently being improved, we are always mindful of the latest trends, trying to understand what the emerging needs might be, or even inventing them, always keeping the whole family in mind.

Other important allies in our commercial model are hotels, with whom we work on two fronts. On the one hand, promoting our products in their vacation clubs, as luxury incentives to reward clients who have bought a hotel membership. On the other hand, selling and promoting our products to their guests.

OUR VISITORS...

91.6% ARE WILLING TO VISIT AND LIVE OUR XPERIENCES AGAIN ON THEIR NEXT TRIP

94.0% BELIEVE THEIR XPERIENCE IN THE PARKS OFFERED VALUE FOR MONEY

99.6% WOULD RECOMMEND THE XPERIENCES WE OFFER TO OTHERS

98/100 THE RATING GIVEN TO THE XPERIENCES OFFERED IN OUR PARKS

In 2009, tickets sold through commercial intermediaries such as travel agencies represented around 80% of our sales; today, they are closer to 50%. Our commercial diversification has been a key factor driving our Group's growth. This was achieved by making our products directly available to tourists, whether through travel agencies, digital platforms, hotels, the internet, social media, our call center, and even on cruises.

Today we have seven parks, a hotel, and offer tours to archaeological sites. Our strategy of selling packages has been crucial, because a tourist can buy two, three, or more park admissions at a better price. Considering that visitors' purchase on average one and a half park admissions, when they buy one of our packages there is no need for them to turn to our competitors—they have all the entertainment for their visit covered.

Even though our main advertising is done by *word of mouth*, these days we put a lot of effort into using digital platforms and social media. Pre-sales have also worked well for us: we offer discounts to people who buy one month or more in advance, which means that when they reach our destination, they are less likely to buy from our competitors because they have already bought our products.

We are opening sales kiosks at airports and shopping centers as well. At present we have more than 50 in Mexico City and other major cities in the country. We are bringing our brands closer to prospective tourists. Although they could already find us on their cell phones or computers, now they can also see us at their favorite shopping center, where one of our representatives will help them and where they will get the same pre-sale discounts.

#MUSTDO:

Learn to put your eggs in different baskets...and that all baskets are important.

Over these past years, we generated strategies that allowed us to diversify our commercial channels with the aim of reaching a growing number of people, of promoting our parks in our tourists' countries of origin, and of achieving more sales. We have successfully attracted tourists through our digital channels and by *word of mouth*, which brings the public directly to our internet site or ticket windows. This has increased sales, reducing the transaction cost (via commissions) and substantially improving our profits.

Thinking digitally means thinking from the outside-in, which entails many challenges—even cultural challenges—to many businesses. The key lies in understanding and even anticipating our clients' behavior: how do they search, how do they communicate, how do they buy, how do they enjoy and share what they do, where do they get their inspiration? Digital media certainly helps us approach people in innovative and original ways.

Xcaret's digital presence answers the phone with a smile in its voice, it inspires smiles with a video, and even shows the world our visitors' smiles while visiting our parks in real time.

We have strengthened our Business to Business digital strategy with the help of our commercial allies, who at present allow us to sell in 99 countries, through 4,700 affiliates. This is how we have reached audiences all over the planet with our products. Clients now compare us to parks in the U.S., Europe, and Asia. Xcaret's competition is global, and we've accepted the challenge.

We have also commercialized our products through leading Online Travel Agencies (OTA) in every region of the world, with whom we have direct connections: Expedia, Bestday, Getyourguide, Viator, TripAdvisor, Tiqets, Veltra, Ctrip, Peek, TripGuru, among others. We have established very good partnerships with Facebook and Google; we are one of their main clients in Mexico.

We have websites in several languages that process transactions in 16 different currencies and can be completed using 37 different payment forms. Their security level is unrivalled when it comes to fraud prevention. Users' xperience is what matters most to us, so developing our systems for use on mobile devices has become a priority.

In 2011, we began our social media strategy from scratch. Today, we have more than five million followers on our various social media channels, which have become our platforms for branding, communication, service, marketing, and sales.

In Asia, positioning a website or social media channels is a completely different matter. We began our strategy in this market in 2015; today, we also have a site in Mandarin.

«IT IS NOT WHAT YOU CAN IMAGINE THAT MAKES YOU CREATIVE BUT RATHER WHAT YOU CAN MAKE OTHERS IMAGINE.»

ANONYMOUS

CREATIVE ADVERTISING

Creativity is one of the values guiding our businesses and a major pillar in the development of our marketing department.

For instance, using «X» in the names of our attractions has been paramount to us, it is our signature. Whenever we find a word we can use with this initial letter in our attractions, we register it to prevent others from appropriating our campaign and to avoid being forbidden from using it in the future. Also, to avoid rip-offs, all our products include the caption «by Xcaret», a seal ensuring the quality of the xperience. In the case of Xcaret itself, because it serves as a showcase for our country and to avoid repetition, we added «by México» instead.

I am very proud of the fact that our communications, advertising, and content campaigns have all been created in-house. Our communication and advertising strategy is based on the different moments when we make contact with visitors, beginning with the planning of the trip, the moment of *dreaming*. As for the digital sphere, we have blogs in Spanish and English for each of our brands, and we also create videos that can be watched through our YouTube channels and other platforms. We have created partnerships with outstanding influencers from different countries, and close relationships with foreign media who share their opinion through Op-Eds.

We realize that we could be in a thousand magazines, but what matters most is appearing in those printed media tourists are actually going to see and read on their way, and on the first day of their vacation. That is why we have created a very important resource: *MAP-A*, which is distributed to tourists when they arrive at the airport. From the moment tourists reach their destination, they already know about us and can make plans as soon as they land—the time when they usually make decisions regarding their stay. We have shifted from the idea of merely being an advertiser to that of being a publisher of news, entertaining and culturally enriching material, guides, books, and maps.

We want our advertising to be different and unconventional, so we have even given the billboards on the Cancún-Riviera Maya corridor a makeover. We build our own structures, and we make them visually attractive and entertaining. We want people to remember them, to smile when they see them, or even to be surprised by them. Our efforts earned us the distinction of «Best Outdoor Advertisement», granted by the IAAPA.

We learned not to take things too seriously by introducing a bit of a sense of humor in our campaigns. The first billboard we made was the one that put us on the map, not only in Mexico City, but also in the rest of the country. Its slogan has become emblematic: «When you go to Xcaret, don't forget to visit Cancún.» I also remember printed ads with park animals laughing and asking: «You think Xel-Há is prettier than Xcaret? Ha, ha, ha!» With one park seeming to make fun of another, it was a way of promoting both.

At present, we are developing a virtual reality tool that will enable us to share the xperience of visiting our parks. It will also help us to train travel agents and will be used at travel fairs and on our social media and digital channels. Our own app is a very useful tool, helping us not only to bring our brands closer to the public, but to improve visitors' xperience by allowing them to make the most of their visit to our parks.

We have a Revenue Management department that focuses on our hotels. This team analyzes information to develop strategies that help improve our profitability. In other words, they help us get maximum benefit from sales through targeted pricing policies based on the demand, the channels of distribution, and the buyers.

Clearly, part of the reason for our success and for our rapid market penetration has been that our new products proudly carry the name Xcaret. Thirty years of labor are being harvested in markets where our brand is loved and valued, such as in Mexico and Latin America. And now, Hotel Xcaret México itself is helping us, through its own commercial channels, to open up new markets where customers may not have known about the parks. It is a winning synergy.

SUSTAINABILITY AT
360º AND IN 3D

CHAPTER 10

Contrary to what some people might think, I have the hardest time talking about sustainability. This is because for me, it is not about a science, a theory, or an academic topic I can discuss at length. Instead, I live sustainability on a day-to-day basis in everything I think and everything I do. For me, sustainability is a daily reality.

Grupo Xcaret's sustainability policy centers on two dimensions—internal and external—and on three axes: the *planet*, including the conservation of ecosystems and species and animal welfare; *people*, that is, fostering respect for human dignity, improving the quality of life, and preserving and disseminating our cultural heritage; and *prosperity*, which involves economic performance, responsible commercialization, and the promotion of the Mexican economy and business ethics. My son, David, says:

«Sustainability is a synonym of equilibrium, the perfect balance of benefits between people, the planet, and prosperity. It's like a spinning top, spinning perfectly when it's balanced, but falling as soon as it is lop-sided.»

I remember a very important meeting more than 20 years ago, involving all partners and our families, in a secluded place in Cancún. Led by our consultant, we wanted to define our Group's vision, our philosophy, as well as our new growth strategy for the future. Together, we created the vision that has ruled the Group to this day: being one-of-a-kind in sustainable tourist recreation.

It is very important to mention that in those days, the word *sustainability* was barely used, least of all in a business' vision statement. We did not yet understand how important the term was. But what was certainly clear to us was that we wanted to do things this way, because we liked it and because we were convinced that was the right way to do them.

#ENTRETIP

Sustainability is not a choice, it is the right way. In nature, there are no rewards or punishments, only consequences.

Since the start of our Group, we haven't only emphasized environmental or ecological concerns, we have also given a lot of thought to people: our visitors, our colleagues, and the communities around us. We always knew that we must care not only for our natural resources, but also for the welfare of those people directly or indirectly involved in our businesses. Likewise, we knew that we should also promote prosperity, in other words, the profitability of the business that would allow us to reinvest and support the regional and national economy.

The only change we have ever made to our vision statement was replacing the word «*sustentabilidad*», commonly referring to a system in need of sustaining, with the word «*sostenibilidad*», often referring to a system that is self-sustaining. The latter takes into account the three axes mentioned earlier and widens the ecological and environmental perspective by including ideas such as reducing consumption, recycling waste, using alternative energies, and using resources more efficiently. In other words, doing more with less, taking care of our environment.

Without realizing it, we were born as a socially responsible company. This has been part of our philosophy and is in the DNA of each and every one of our colleagues. Visitors, colleagues, suppliers, local communities, and even policy makers identify our Group as uniquely different, thanks to our transparency and honesty, part of the core values underpinning our origin, our growth, and our present success.

We were taking care of turtles from the very early days and talking about animal welfare long before that concept was widely used. We were helping communities when no enterprise would look their way. We recovered cultural traditions that were starting to disappear, we planted trees in the central ridges of the road when not even the government would do it. We improved roadways and even built the first phase of a bicycle lane network which will soon reach Cancún. We supported civil organizations from many spheres. All this because we thought it was the right thing to do, the necessary thing, and because we were convinced that it was the only way for our own environment and company to evolve. We cannot just sit around waiting for the proper authorities to solve everything.

That is why when I'm asked about sustainability, I cannot answer with technical terms. But what I can do is recommend both to companies and to people to be congruent: congruent in everything they are thinking, saying, and doing. Be congruent with nature, be congruent with the people around you, and be congruent with prosperity, which should be fostered by your own creativity. This is the only way to be sustainable: creating a never-ending virtuous circle. It is not about installing solar panels or recycling waste. We must look beyond, think of others, turn to look at everyone and at everything around us. Taking actions that have to do with your business' nature is true sustainability, because that is where we can make a difference.

When deciding what to invest in, or who to invest with, we must consider those who are in the same sustainability boat. One must be aware of who to support and who not to support, who to buy from and who not to buy from; it is not about rewarding those who are doing well, or punishing those who are doing badly, but rather about everyone becoming aware. We must do sustainability over 360° and in 3D—in every direction, with your clients, your suppliers, your colleagues, your neighbors, your community, your country, the environment, and the entire world.

#MUSTBE:

**Sustainability must be done
over 360° and in third dimension.**

Many people ask me: «Why bother building stone walls when the brick ones cost only a third of the price?» I always answer,

«Quality pays off, and brings the biggest returns.» Finally, sustainable actions also contribute to your competitive edge. When we develop projects, the fact that they will generate development and well-being through their economic spillover is guaranteed from the start: work, revenue, quality, service, and a reduced environmental impact—it's very likely they will be followed by success.

One of our greatest contributions is to teach our suppliers, colleagues, and visitors, in the flesh, that development and sustainability are not at odds, they can walk in tandem, hand-in-hand. For us, sustainability is not a choice, it's the only way. Those who have not integrated sustainability into their vision statement are destined to disappear in the short run.

#MUSTBE:

**Those who have not embraced
sustainability are destined to disappear.**

In 2020 our organization celebrated its third decade of existence. Ever since it was born, we have worked to have a profitable business which enables us to invest the necessary resources in social and environmental causes. In our parks, however, we have identified a change in the pattern of tourists' habits: they prefer sustainable destinations, hotel developments and entertainment companies that follow environmentally sound practices that benefit communities. To some extent, I think that is why they prefer us.

A PLACE WE CALL «HOME»

We need to think about what will happen to our planet and to us in the future, how we will tackle global warming and the ever-growing production of waste, and what we will do to restore our flora and fauna. That is why we have taken different actions that help take care of our environment.

We use a lot of fuel for our vehicles. To avoid causing long queues at the gas stations, we used to refuel our 200 buses at dawn in Playa del Carmen. Each one has a 105-gallon gas tank. To decrease the amount of diesel we use daily, we opened our own gas station at Xcaret, not because we are interested in the gas business—it's really for our own supply—but because it reduces consumption by hundreds of daily gallons, simply by not having to travel back and forth. Our carbon footprint automatically decreases, one small step at a time.

WE RECYCLE ✚ THAN **80%** OF OUR SOLID WASTE

In all our parks, tours, and hotels we implement a solid waste separation program. We separate waste meticulously in our Transfer and Collection Centers. We deliver the solid waste we recover to authorized independent suppliers for its proper treatment—mostly, it is destined to be recycled. The profit obtained from the sale of these products is granted to Flora, Fauna y Cultura de México, A. C., so they can use it for their various programs. As for organic waste, we make compost, which can be used as substrate in the breeding programs of native plants in our nurseries. By also adding soil into our land and with our irrigation system, our gardens have turned into a luscious garden.

We had to clear our properties of *waaxiim*, a very harmful and invasive type of acacia shrub, which takes advantage of the jungle's weakened condition after hurricanes to spread. Fortunately, in time, we eliminated this plague and replanted native flora that had disappeared.

We take advantage of all our resources: by having nurseries, being good gardeners, and breeding the threatened native flora of Quintana Roo, we contribute to the reforestation of the region. A year ago, we decided to take responsibility for planting the whole length of the central ridge on the highway from Cancún to Tulum, which had been mostly barren or abandoned. It is a four-year reforestation project. We believe that if you are a baker, you should give away bread. When you share your own resources, the things you produce, it costs half as much and gives you twice the return. That highway is the most symbolic garden in the Cancún-Riviera Maya region, it is our facade, the frontage to all our hotels, the first and the last thing that our visitors see.

«YOU'LL NEVER GET A SECOND CHANCE TO MAKE A GOOD FIRST IMPRESSION.»

ANONYMOUS

#MUSTDO:

If you're a baker, give away bread. When you share your own resources, the things you produce, it costs half as much and gives you twice the return.

KEEPING AN EYE ON WATER

Our commitment to water conservation and the conservation of the life forms inhabiting the underground rivers, the mangroves, the xenotes, the beaches, and coves is supported by an awareness-raising program about the use of chemical-free sunscreens. Through our sales channels we point out the importance of using these products to ensure we are taking care of the water through our xperiences. Our commercial partners support us in raising awareness among our visitors.

WE HAND OUT
200 000
200 000 FREE SAMPLES OF CHEMICAL-FREE SUNSCREENS TO OUR VISITORS EVERY YEAR IN EXCHANGE FOR THEIR PERSONAL COMMERCIAL SUNSCREEN.

The parks have their own wastewater and reverse-osmosis water treatment plants to produce drinkable water for humans. Through these processes, we avoid polluting the aquifers in the region, which are very fragile due to their karst topology. The water we recover is used inside our parks to care for our green areas. We have also implemented efficient water use systems such as waterless urinals, water efficient showers, and low flow taps and toilets, all routinely maintained.

Our next step is to reduce the number of single-use plastic water and soda bottles. We are moving towards ensuring our parks are ready so that visitors can simply refill their water bottles when they need to, instead of indiscriminately throwing away bottles. This project was extremely urgent and important to us, therefore we implemented it in January 2020.

We want to promote this project beyond our own parks, by convincing and collaborating with the authorities so that small reverse osmosis water treatment plants are built in public spaces, such as archaeological sites, to make water drinkable and available to all visitors through drinking fountains. At Hotel Xcaret México, all water bottles are now made of glass. It is time for the industry to go green.

ELECTRIC ENERGY

Another great accomplishment was becoming more efficient energy consumers. Right now, we are innovating by implementing effective engineering solutions that are integrated into our electromechanical installations. Gradually, we have installed technology that helps us properly manage our electric energy consumption. This technology used to be either unavailable or very costly. Among the things we have implemented are the following:

In our hotels, we are installing intelligent smart control systems so that climate and lighting, among other functions, are monitored and regulated automatically.

In our hotels and parks, we have installed «chillers» to dispense ice-cold water. We have set them up in a non-conventional manner that has resulted in savings of up to 30 percent.

All our lighting is last-generation technology, saving up to 86% in energy use compared to incandescent or halogen lamps. Also, in most cases, these fixtures are dimmable, allowing for regulation of the intensity of the light.

In some areas, we have installed water pumps with very low power consumption. They use a permanent magnet generator, similar to the one found in hybrid cars, which has resulted in energy savings of up to 90% compared to conventional pumps. Yes, we only use 10% of what we might use by conventional standards.

For our swimming pools, we have installed salt-based chlorine makers which provide an efficient disinfection treatment free of chemical compounds. By making our own chlorine on-site, we no longer need to buy chlorine produced in chemical processing plants elsewhere, which helps to reduce the energy use and emissions from production, packaging, transportation, and storage. Since the chlorine we make is pure, we do not have to worry about the strong odor, the itchy eyes, and the irritated skin typically caused by the additives in bottled chlorine.

With these actions, we are helping to address climate change. We are also fostering the production and use of renewable, clean and sustainable energy that avoids releasing contaminants and greenhouse gases. By the end of 2021, all the electric energy consumed by Grupo Xcaret will be renewable.

SPECIES CONSERVATION PROGRAMS

Two years after opening Xcaret, in 1992, we started our first conservation projects. At first, we began by merely showing the native flora and fauna, hoping to make visitors more aware of it. This required a group of technicians and professionals in the field to care for and breed our species. As a result of our daily controls and statistics, we gathered a lot of information. Armed with this wealth of data and species, we knew it was our responsibility to take things even further. That is why we decided to create different endangered species protection programs, with the support of our people and their xpertise.

Although we do not aspire to become a science institute, we do provide support for specialized researchers, shelter for rescued or injured animals, staff support to various institutions, and allow for certain operations and tests to be run in our facilities, since here we have the raw material and the equipment. Our gain is threefold: we exhibit, breed, and conserve. In fact, we have a very close relationship with the federal Office for Environmental Protection (PROFEPA), with which we work collaboratively.

In Xcaret, we have a unique aviary: it is a huge valley with a xenote inside and a vast net up above which allows birds to have plenty of space to fly. Several natural habitats were created: the high jungle (the rainforest), the lowlands (sub-deciduous), the cloud forest, the mangrove, the wetland, the semi-arid area, and the shrubland zone. This aviary has an incubator area for the breeding of macaws and flamingos, and a raptor bird area.

825 SPECIMENS FROM A TOTAL OF

67 DIFFERENT SPECIES

IN A SURFACE OF **3 000** SQUARE YARDS

In 1993, we spontaneously began the macaw breeding program with a pair of macaws sold to us by a friend from Cancún, who also taught us how to breed them. In 2014, a survey was carried out to find out how many macaws were living in the wild in Mexico—there were around 250. By then, we already had about one thousand in Xcaret, many more than what we needed in the park for the free flying macaw attraction done twice a day—we release 50 at a time, allowing them to fly freely over the park before returning soon after by themselves. In our incubators, 150 are born every year. We had to keep our own numbers under control, so we asked for permission to release them into the wild in Chiapas and Veracruz. We got permission in 2016. To this day, we have released more than 250 live macaws into the jungle, with an adaptation and survival rate of 92%. We get a lot of satisfaction from these actions, not only because we have doubled this species' population, but also because we have already had sightings of nests from the birds we released. We are proud *grandmacaws*!

WE INCREASED THE WILD POPULATION OF SCARLET MACAWS IN MEXICO BY

100%

Since removing flamingos from their natural habitat is forbidden in Mexico, we brought our first 20 specimens from Cuba in exchange for macaws. Today we have 120, and around 23 more are born every year. We once rescued 200 eggs left by their mothers when a jaguar came into their nesting ground in Ría Lagartos, Yucatán. Once they were born, we had to hand-feed them every three hours using droppers. We had to get some helping hands—adoptive mothers—and managed to enlist university students from all over the world; we took care of the rest. Half of these birds were reintroduced to their natural habitat, while the other half was donated to zoos and aviaries around the world.

The macaw and flamingo breeding programs have been very successful. Our toucan program is still in its trial period.

Regarding sea animals, the white turtle and the logger-head sea turtle are in danger of extinction, mainly because inhabitants from the communities near the coast used to eat their meat and eggs. We created the largest sea turtle con-servation program in the region, which allows us to monitor their return to the sea. We have the only certified sea turtle hospital. Nowadays, the turtles even have to take a number and wait their turn!

So far, we have had two generations of sea turtles return-ing to their place of birth to bury their own eggs in the sand, an average of 150 each time. We know this because we have a hatchling marking program. The sea turtles' carapace is divided into different polygonal sections called scutes which we have numbered for each species. We make a small circu-lar notch in the hatchlings' abdominal area, which is white, and exchange it with a similar sized fragment cut from their carapace, which is a bit darker. As these grafts heal, they are quickly integrated into the tissue. Every year we make these grafts in a specific part of the carapace. Therefore, when they return as adults—usually after 15 years—we immediately know what year they were released into the sea. We feel like mother hens waiting for their chicks to swim back home to our beaches every year.

15 MILLION
SEA TURTLE HATCHLINGS HAVE
BEEN RELEASED SINCE 1993

350
VOLUNTEERS PROVE
SUPPORT IN THE SEA
TURTLE CAMPS

We started taking in manatees rescued by the authorities after they were injured or stranded. Now we breed them in the park. Today, we are the parents of five manatees born at home.

As for the flora, we have a forest nursery, where we grow native plants—mostly endemic or endangered species— besides orchids, bromeliads, and helicons. Our mangrove reforestation and rehabilitation program—unique in the country—has also borne fruit. We have been reforesting a large portion of the Nichupté Lagoon System in Cancún for 10 years and the protected natural area on Cozumel island for five years.

SINCE 2018 WE'VE REFORESTED

494 ACRES OF MANGROVE

123 ACRES OF COASTAL LAGOONS IN COZUMEL

172 ACRES IN THE NICHUPTÉ LAGOON IN CANCÚN

7 413 161 ACRES OF TREES AND PALM TREES HAVE BEEN PLANTED IN

20 YEARS

To take advantage of the coral reefs in our coastal properties, we designed one of only three living coral reef aquariums in the world. One of our greatest technical accomplishments was bringing sea water containing plankton—the microscopic organisms on which corals feed—through pipes stretching 1640 feet out to sea that are perfectly secured to the bottom of the sea so they will not be dragged off by strong tides during hurricane season.

We have succeeded in reintroducing elkhorn coral colonies in affected areas of the reefs, though finding and training specialized personnel has been a challenge.

«ALONE YOU GO FAST, BUT TOGETHER WE GO FURTHER.»
ANONYMOUS

A LABOR OF LOVE WILL TAKE YOU FAR ABOVE

We had a clear starting point, a mission shared across the entire organization. One of the reasons behind our success is our determination to get things right from the start; another is the uniqueness of our products; yet another is the talented team that provides them, and offers our customers an xcellent service. To accomplish this, one needs to have happy colleagues, excellent hosts, hospitable, helpful, and well-trained. Inside our organization, we have an xperienced team imagining and proposing new things every day. They are at the front line, training their sights on continuous improvement, optimization, and uniqueness, all within a framework of service and quality. In tandem, we have a team of executives, most of whom have been in their positions between 10 and 20 years, providing stability, solidity, and cohesion to the company.

There are more than 8 000 of us working in the parks, tours, and the hotel, plus those who are on the construction site, building our future. Now that Xavage has opened, we hired more than 350 new colleagues, and in our next hotel—already under construction—we will be needing another 1500. We are lucky to have so much more work left to do.

Surround yourself with the best people available to lead your business. A business is only as good as the people it employs. And not only that, you must place everyone in the right place, both for you and for them. If they are not the right fit, do not conform, do not waste your time or theirs. Remove them at once and do not stop until you have found the right person for the right job. Not until you have accomplished this will you be able to claim victory and attend to the other more important point in your business: your product.

Try to integrate your team of executives with colleagues from different fields, with different ways of thinking, so they complement each other. Neither you nor anyone can know everything. If two people think alike, one can be spared.

While you are building your team, the turnover of personnel does not matter. You will not see results until you have fully assembled your team, with a clear direction, training, and leadership. Once that all is in place, before you know it you will be heading where you wanted to go, and beyond.

Perhaps, when starting your business you were afraid of falling on hard and hungry times. Once you have managed to create a unique product you are passionate about, have consolidated your team as described above, and given it clear objectives and a sense of direction, you may still be at risk of dying—not of hunger, but of indigestion.

#ENTREPTIP:

We must surround ourselves with the best people; an excellent talented human team is our greatest strength.

Fifteen years ago, many hoteliers would approach our well-trained—and therefore highly coveted—staff when they were off work, often as they were leaving the park, with the intention of poaching them. They would do this quite simply by asking them how much they earned, and then offering them twice as much, easy as that. Today, they keep trying to do the same, but our collaborators do not leave anymore. Here, they share in the values that have given them a sense of roots and loyalty to the company, a sense of belonging. Money is no longer the primary motivation. They are doing something they like, and they feel safe in our company, in our family. They trust us. Grupo Xcaret is the miracle of many human beings evolving together, a human team developing with the Group.

When hurricane Emily hit in 2005, it passed through the area in only two hours. Damage was limited and recovery was quick. Two months later, hurricane Wilma spent two whole days devastating the area. It slammed us with gale-force winds of the highest intensity as it inched its way across the region. It did what it pleased with us, with disastrous consequences.

Hotels started rebuilding and most of them fired their operative staff. People discovered they were out of a job when they saw their names on sheets of paper stuck onto the doors at their places of work. All the families in the area were very concerned. In our case, we had to close for fifty days, because all our palapas had been blown away by the hurricane. Demand to visit our parks has always been high, but with all other attractions closed, the few tourists who stayed in the region wanted to go to our parks: it was our duty to open as soon as possible.

«TALENT WINS GAMES, BUT TEAMWORK AND INTELLIGENCE WINS CHAMPIONSHIPS.»

MICHAEL JORDAN

The situation was critical, but we found a compromise. Partners and staff from Xel-Há and Xcaret gathered together in a large hall. We built up the courage to say:

«We know the overall picture for our destination and for ourselves is grave. To survive, so that we do not lose our jobs and can keep our clients, we're going the extra mile not to fire anyone, but we need everyone's help and sacrifice. We've decided to lower wages on a scale from 10% to 50%, depending on the position and the salary, so that we have the lesser effect on those who make lower wages. We don't know how long this will last. If anyone thinks they won't be able to withstand it, we suggest they collect their severance pay in our offices. We have no other choice. Otherwise, we would have to close the park.»

We have never received a louder and longer round of applause than the one our colleagues gave us that day. We told them we would pay them half their wages, and there they were, on their feet, giving us a heart-felt round of applause. Everyone expected to be out of a job, like so many of all the other families in the region, but Grupo Xcaret was different, we were all in the same boat, and we all needed each other. I get goosebumps just remembering that moment.

We have learned that conflicts, problems, and challenging situations—like an epidemic, a hurricane, or public safety concerns—bring people together in solidarity and unity to help us find a solution.

With fair wages, the right jobs, and good benefits, we have brought about trust and security in our colleagues, happy people. Even under the worst circumstances, including hurricanes, they know they will not lose their jobs. We solve our problems together, because they are everyone's problems, and we are one family. How can a person with a family to support carry on if they do not know how long his job will last? How happy can they be as they go about their job every day? If you can achieve job security, you are likely to work twice as hard.

When we notice that a colleague is not happy, we try to reassign him to another role he might enjoy more. If that does not work, and we have already tried everything unsuccessfully, we will even help him find a new job elsewhere! We must help people find their vocation, to give meaning to their lives, to make them feel useful, to bring the Group's way of being—our DNA—into their homes, to integrate it into their daily lives. We want people who can smile at life every day, because only then can they truly greet our visitors with a big smile.

«NO ONE IS SO POOR THAT THEY CANNOT GIVE A SMILE, NOR SO RICH THAT THEY CAN DO WITHOUT IT.»

ANONYMOUS

Our in-house team of builders, comprising 400 to 500 workers and craftsmen, used to work from Monday through Saturday. Most of them live in different towns in Yucatán, so on Saturday nights—pay day—they would get home very late. Consequently, they only rested on Sunday, and on Monday at the crack of dawn were getting ready to go back to the construction site. I felt we had to do something about it, so we decided to extend the working day by one hour from Monday to Friday, thus reducing the working week to five days and freeing the weekend. This measure meant they could be with their families Saturdays and Sundays. Imagine that: it is not just one extra day, it is twice the amount of time with their families, a radical change of life.

Some years ago, we conducted a poll asking how much our colleagues paid for mobile phone services. On average, they spent MX $400 a month. We talked to the phone company, Telcel, and secured a plan that cost less than a quarter of the average cost. We signed a contract to acquire handsets for all our colleagues. This way, we could provide them with a good benefit, which also happens to be an excellent tool for work and a means to be in direct contact, especially in case of an emergency. By doing so, we also helped them make savings on that monthly expense, which meant more cash availability. It was as if we had given them a MX $400 raise. Later, we extended this plan to their family members, getting 25% more additional phone lines. In those cases, the amount was discounted from the applicant's paycheck.

«THE MOST PRODUCTIVE WORK COMES FROM THE HANDS OF A HAPPY PERSON.»

VÍCTOR PAUCHET

In a similar fashion, we helped colleagues living in areas that our staff shuttles did not reach save close to MX $600 a month. They once paid MX $18 every day for public transportation—riding on a «pesero»—that took them to Xcaret's shuttle stops. Eventually, we got the municipality to authorize an extension of our routes, and we managed for the taxis and «pesero» unions to work with us, which meant more comfort and savings in transportation and time for our people.

One of our missions is to have our colleagues regain their wage's purchasing power. What is the use of giving them a 4% raise, following a 4% inflation rate? The next day, everyone raises prices, rendering the raise in wages null. We have been adjusting our wages by at least 25% above the inflation rate, and looking for more ways for our colleagues to get more and to legally pay fewer deductions.

«WHEN YOU SHARE WEALTH, YOU ARE LEFT WITH HALF; WHEN YOU SHARE KNOWLEDGE, YOU ARE LEFT WITH TWICE AS MUCH.»

ANONYMOUS

In the field of education, we added our efforts to those of the «Cero Rezago Educativo» (No Educational Lag), a national program promoting adult literacy. When we started Xcaret, many of our colleagues could not read or write. The program's goal was to teach reading and writing and to allow members of staff who hadn't done so to finish primary school. We later decided to take this further and help people finish secondary school. Today, those colleagues who haven't finished their basic education can catch up with their studies in our parks. We also have scholarship agreements and university grants. Our executives are tasked with motivating their teams to finish their university studies and pursue graduate studies. We reward being motivated to continue studying and advancing. Also, all colleagues receive institutional, strategic, and technical training, and have the possibility of getting xcellence scholarships for their children.

In the state of Quintana Roo, we are the company that most often hires people who have never worked before. What others consider a disadvantage, due to someone's lack of xperience, we consider an advantage; we can train them, in our own way, in the field for which they are best suited that is most convenient for us, and they are free of foibles and bad habits.

We also have an educational program that promotes the protection and conservation of Quintana Roo's natural and cultural heritage. The program offers thematic tours about climate change, endangered flora and fauna ecosystems, best environmental practices, responsible tourism, and Maya culture. Every year, we receive more than fourteen thousand primary school students and teachers from 300 public schools in the state, thanks to an agreement signed with the Ministry of Education and Culture in the state of Quintana Roo.

#ENTREPTIP:

Let us improve the development and well-being of our colleagues, their families, and the community. We must foster their improvement with good examples, knowledge, training, culture, sports, entertainment, benefits, and opportunities.

Due to the seasonal nature of Mexico's tourist industry, many companies do not register their workers with the Mexican Social Security Institute (IMSS). There are usually intermediaries or payment agencies who manage their payroll. Grupo Xcaret is one of the few companies that has all members of staff on the payroll, registered with IMSS, and with a consolidated daily wage, so they can get all social security benefits stipulated by law, plus our benefits. In a country where the opposite is often the norm, being honest with people is not often an accepted value—until you find yourself working for a company that makes following the rules an essential part of its nature, of its way of being.

Once, while hiring personnel for the hotel, the Human Talent director was updating us on the registration status of our staff with Social Security Institute. Another recently employed executive interrupted him to suggest that we should not do that, as it was an unnecessary expense. The answer was: «This is how we do things.» End of discussion.

Some companies let people go during low season. We try not to let anyone go: our collaborators have to eat every day, not seasonally. This has to do with respecting people, being loyal and ethical. You cannot stop paying a gardener because it has not rained or because the grass has not grown enough—the gardener must still bring home some earnings every day. Either you integrate it into your expenses, or you stop paying for the service altogether. We must never undermine human dignity. While the average staff turnover in the region is over 80%, ours is only 22%.

On the other hand, there is the question of technologies that have been replacing many functions previously carried out by humans. I welcome technology to make processes more efficient, but not to displace people; we are not disposable. The human soul, heart, and spirit are irreplaceable. We are reaching a stage where we may be using technology as an excuse to justify immoral behaviors in the interest of productivity. We have greater wealth and less human dignity. Money is costing us dearly.

«OPEN YOUR ARMS TO CHANGE, BUT DON'T LET GO OF YOUR VALUES.»

DALAI LAMA

For many people, success is about accumulating money. For others, it is about being famous. For me, it is about achieving happiness. Happiness is a choice. When it comes to choosing a career path or a project, you must choose whatever makes you feel fulfilled. If you do what you love, it is very likely that you will do it well. In my case, after twenty amazing years as a shopkeeper, all my passions converged in a single project: Xcaret. Here, the more I do, the happier I am.

«WE WERE BORN FOR HAPPINESS, EVERYTHING ELSE IS BESIDE THE POINT.»

FACUNDO CABRAL

#MUSTBE:

For many people, success is about accumulating money; for others, it is about being famous; for me, it is about achieving happiness.

VIRTUOUS CIRCLES

Every task begins at home: first, you help your family; then, your business, your neighbors, your community, and your country. There are problems all over the world, but making your contribution closer to home is more efficient. Paying for freight and fuel costs cancels out any environmental benefits we try to achieve, which is why we look for local suppliers. When we cannot find what we want locally, we look for it elsewhere in the country. We rarely import products from abroad, it is our last resource. A case in point are our shops at Xcaret, where we do not sell foreign products. There are no Milky Way or Snickers chocolate bars. Instead, we have national brands: Tin Larín, Carlos V, Escalona, to name only a few. We have uniforms made locally, never further than in Chiapas or Oaxaca. Consuming local products first, and then national ones, is one of our main contributions to the region's sustainability.

31% REST OF THE COUNTRY

8% YUCATÁN

60% QUINTANA ROO

1% OTHER COUNTRIES

42% BIG COMPANIES

13% MEDIUM-SIZED COMPANIES

45% SMALL COMPANIES

What interests us is promoting the growth and development of vulnerable communities in the region. Our hotel is a good example. For three years, we have been going back and forth between different towns in Campeche, where artisans hand-weave the small *jipijapa* palm baskets we fill with tradi-tional Mexican sweets and leave in our guests' rooms every evening. At first, we acquired 80; the next month, 120; then it was 130. Today, as many as 18,000 are ready for us to collect every month. At the moment, we need 900 each day at the hotel. When we open our new developments, we will need many more. It is a similar story with the salsas and jams for our hotel restaurants, the toiletries for our bathrooms, and even some liquors for the hotel bars. All are local products, made by local workers using ingredients from the Yucatán peninsula.

At first, our profit margin is small because the artisans cannot issue the right paperwork that might make the purchases tax-deductible for us, but we work with them to get them up-and-running, always prioritizing their daily welfare. Once they are on track, we help them register with the tax authorities. I want each of them to develop; we help them, train them, equip them, and even ask them to invite their neighbors to join in as our suppliers.

#ENTREPTIP:

**Think globally, buy locally. Let us show
solidarity with Mexico by consuming
what the country produces.**

I find it very endearing to be asked the same question every time I visit these small towns: «Tell us, how long is this going to last?» «All your life», I reply. These types of actions are increasing and now many people depend on our Group. That is why I tell my children, my successors, that they cannot meddle with this concept. We have a huge responsibility, and if they change the approach, they will have to teach these artisans a new and similarly dignified way to sustain themselves.

«A RICH MAN IS NOT HE WHO HAS MORE, BUT HE WHO NEEDS LESS.»

ANONYMOUS

Personally, hearing that 99% of the wealth is owned by 1% of the population poses a dilemma for me. I am on the side of entrepreneurial capitalism, as long as we are talking about socially conscious, just, responsible, and sustainable businesses. I mean businesses with a good return on investment, but also generating jobs, paying taxes, repaying society, and whose profits are aimed at promoting continued growth and activating the region's economy. It is not assets that make people rich, but the good use they put those assets to.

What is criminal is businesses generating profits in Mexico and sending them abroad, refusing to foster the development of the country where they made those profits to begin with. Money is round for a reason: so that it can roll, creating economic spillover, reinvestment and production, as close to home as possible. Yes, we must aim at distributing profit more fairly among those who made it, but also among locals. It is using wealth that generates wealth, not its ownership.

#MUSTBE:

You do not have to be a millionaire to be rich, just be generous.

XCARET IS A STATE OF MIND

Macaws are such charismatic birds
that, when released into the wild,
they also release consciousness. The
macaw's reintroduction program is
one of the most successful of its kind
in Mexico.

Rotating panoramic ▶
tower in Cancún:
380 ft in height.

◀ Selling copies of the
first issue of **Reforma
Cancún** newspaper,
just as it was done by
volunteer newsvendors
when the paper
launched in Mexico City.

◀ We had a very tight
advertising budget for
my social enterprise,
Mucha Leche. I had
to do some of the
modelling myself.

▼ **Cancún Theater** is the
only theater in the city
so far.

From folksy to sophisticated. Our old-fashioned buses provide transportation to Cancún and the Riviera Maya. They are adorned with turkeys, sacks of grain, fruit and vegetables, and have reclining seats and air conditioning. The *kukulcanes* are more sophisticated, and able to undertake longer cross-state journeys. They have separated ladies and gentlemen's toilets.

NATURE'S SACRED PARADISE

XCARET
C A N C U N

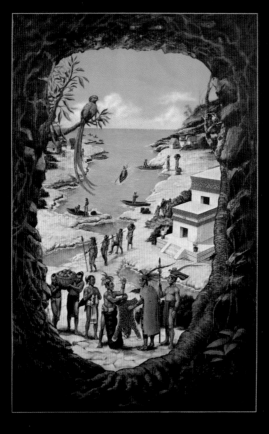

◄ Our **first promotional poster**, also used for our brochure covers, shows the inlet in the old port of Polé—now Xcaret.

Our **most successful promotional poster** became an important icon. Today, we also use this design for towels and clothing in our stores. ►

Xotic, Xciting, one of our most creative campaigns, promoted through 12 different billboards along the highway from Cancún to Tulum. ◄

▲ *XCARET, A PARK WITH MANY...BIRTHS.*

▲ *WHO SAID XEL-HÁ IS PRETTIER THAN XCARET?*

Xel-Há's Scenic Lighthouse is another example of our ►
«Yes, we can do it!» philosophy. As a lighthouse in Xel-Há's port, it
has become a landmark. It also has a practical use: it offers
a panoramic view of the sea, with the added bonus of being
the most fun descent from any lighthouse. All this, without ruining
the spirit of the natural wonder that is Xel-Há.

Xavage originated in a *sascabera*, an open mine of limestone gravel (*sascab*), which had been turned into a dump site. Today, after being restored, cleaned up, and reforested, it is an adventure park during the day, and the **Xoximilco** park at night.

A bird's eye view of **Hotel Xcaret México**.

Xibalbá integrates nine of the most attractive xenotes in the state of Yucatán into a single route. It is our first park in this beautiful state.

A GOOD ROOSTER
CAN CROW ANYWHERE

CHAPTER 11

FISCAL HURRICANE

By 2014, we had grown exponentially. We already had six parks and tours to archaeological sites. We had the wind in our sails, until we got hit by a different type of hurricane: the fiscal reform. After passing a tax reform law, the federal government began implementing various changes that would gravely affect our cash flow.

- The value-added tax or IVA, a consumption tax for border regions, increased from 11% to 16%, which, in turn, raised our prices to the public by 5%, resulting in a drop in tourist numbers.
- Tax deduction on investments was eliminated, resulting in a substantial increase in income tax or ISR from

one year to the next compared to what was paid in previous years, directly affecting our reinvestment strategy.

- Social security deductions associated with a savings fund and food vouchers, among others, were restricted. This automatically increased our spending per member of staff and decreased our colleagues' purchasing power.
- The payroll tax increased by 50%.

Just as I have told you about the opportunities brought about by hurricanes for rebuilding oneself and becoming stronger, this fiscal hurricane turned into another major challenge, forcing us to reinvent ourselves to be able to continue our growth. We needed to do some reengineering.

My sole xperience with this type of restructuring dated from 14 years ago, when Marcos, one of my partners, hired a firm from Mexico City specializing in organizational reengineering. All I remember from this xperience is being given, after a month's worth of analysis, a list of things we should eliminate or stop doing, mainly in the product area, at the heart of our business. Most of them were small, but there was one that set off alarm bells for me: we were told we had to get rid of the guitarist and singer who performed three 45-minute sets a day in the open amphitheater, right next to the underground river. The reason, we were told, was that there were never more than 15 people watching and listening to him sing in the amphitheater. He was a costly and underused asset.

My only intervention was to point out their limited vision and lack of sensitivity about this matter, as in most of their other recommendations. The musician was sitting just off center, at the edge of the stage, three feet from the park's main underground river, down which over two thousand visitors slowly floated every day. Notwithstanding that he would have his back to them, the musician delights floating passersby for several magical minutes before they reach him, and for many more as they float away, as they drift along the park's wonderful caverns. His audience was not only the handful of people sitting on the stands, it was also those two thousand people charmed by his music while swimming nearby. The reengineering technicians did not share our DNA, they did not see what we saw, and they could not do the job only we could do. Needless to say, they did not last much longer on the project.

The lesson learned is an important one. One can only reengineer from the inside out, not the other way around. It must be done mainly in-house, following the company's goal, vision, and philosophy, its DNA. Any external consultation must be restricted to methodology and recommendations.

This time, to *grab the bull by the horns*, we did thorough teamwork, following these three guidelines:

1. Identify whatever was not adding any value and stop doing it.
2. Identify what we were doing right and do more of it.
3. Identify what we were not doing yet and start doing it.

At first, it was a difficult process, because we had to recognize our need to eliminate things, practices, attractions, or processes we liked, or that made us feel comfortable, but had become a dead weight. We found duplicated functions. We found different practices in the parks focusing on similar situations and seized the opportunity to standardize the most efficient ones. Finally, we found areas of opportunity and efficiency right under our noses that we had not been able to detect before.

As part of the reengineering process, after analyzing some candidates' strengths, weaknesses, and competences, especially considering our future growth, I took the last step towards the final integration of Grupo Xcaret: I appointed Xel-Há park's Director, a lady, as Executive Director of all operations in all our parks and tours. We needed to consolidate all the parks under one *umbrella*, allowing us to make sure they were *all rowing in the same direction*, towards the same objectives and principles, while generating economies of scale.

With this major step, we concluded the corporatization process, laying the ground for our future growth and consolidating a great executive team, integrated by two women and one man, all of them young, talented, brilliant, with excellent careers ahead of them, and committed to the bone to Grupo Xcaret's DNA. They, in turn, lead a solid and consistent team of executives, which is now beginning to shape the Group's future generations.

To some, it seemed at first a painful exercise, but the reengineering was necessary: removing the fat and leaving only the lean muscle to sustain ourselves and be able to keep growing. I myself had to set aside some favorite projects I had begun years back, like the mushroom farm, the aquaculture and hydroponics project, closing our warehouse and purchasing office in Mexico City, doing without external consulting services, among others, whose cost-benefit relation was no longer justified. The whole process was a lesson in humility.

This effort was absolutely worth it. We finished 2014 with close to a 5% increase in number of visitors and a 12% increase in net income. We kept our costs and expenses 3% below planned expenditure, we maintained our colleagues' purchasing power, and succeeded in increasing the Group's profitability by 4%; all this in spite of the fiscal reform.

Reengineering came to stay. Now, it is an integral part of our daily lives, through self-criticism, continuous improvement, and optimization of processes. We succeeded in making everyone a part of our efforts at efficiency and efficacy, at being thrifty without sacrificing quality, and at attaining better results by doing more with less. This is how we have made sure to remain agile, flexible, and on the cutting edge, always ready for the future.

CROSSING THE LINE WITHOUT CROSSING IT

Regarding our parks, we have two courses of action: improving the products we already have and developing new ones. Since the Group has kept growing, we have all kinds of expenses and more than half of the resources we generate go to operations, maintenance, renovations, and extensions. Last year, we built new shelters for our macaws, and now it is time to expand our warehouses, freezers, and other storage spaces. We have to replace our buses, which are already depreciated and obsolete, and in response to our annual growth, we have to buy more so that we can transport the increasing number of visitors. All this besides maintaining our infrastructure, the areas the public does not see. It is about using resources wisely. But how to prioritize?

Every product has a life span, but our competitors are quick in coming up with other attractions, so we need to refresh our product, give it a real boost. That is why, as I have said before, we always survey our customers, asking for their opinions for improvement and their suggestions, and we really pay attention. It is the customers who, with their views and perceptions, set the real standards of quality. We sell solutions, not products; visitors do not buy a specific product, they buy the whole company, they want to commit to it.

In the case of Xel-Há, which already offered an «all in-clusive» package, the day we opened the new scenic lighthouse and water slide was a turning point. Every year, survey results showed that customers wanted slides and amusement park rides, even though that was not our thing. The Group has its own culture and philosophy and I am quite strict about not getting off the road we have planned. However, we had to think of ways to show that we could in fact do it, to satisfy our visitors' demands without breaking our own rule about being a natural park, not a water park or an amusement park.

Since Xel-Há is a large inlet, it was an important Maya shel-tering port, a wide door to the sea with small interior coves. Pre-Hispanic canoes and small vessels came here to pro-tect themselves from inclement weather, especially storms and hurricanes. All along the coast, every 1,640 feet, there are ancient 13 ft x 13 ft construction sites that used to light up the edge of the coast with torches, as well as the small inlets and ports. Accordingly, building a modern-day light-house in Xel-Há was 100% justified. Reproducing a Maya lighthouse, however, was not an option for us. It would be 131 feet tall, offering a 360-degree panoramic view of the astonishing blue of the Mexican Caribbean Sea, the inlet, and the jungle. This way, visitors would not need to lift their eyes to find heaven.

Lighthouses are usually painted in candy-cane colored stripes. Ours would have a central spiral staircase to go up, and to add some fun to it, we designed four waterslides each with different speed levels to go down. Of course, once up there, no one wants to go down the stairs. With this solution, we do not have slides; this is our natural way of descending from this viewpoint. Even in our lighthouse signs throughout the park, it is identified as «Scenic Lighthouse», never as a waterslide. The trick is to solve problems as they occur, without crossing the line; in this case, maintaining the concept of a natural park.

#MUSTDO:

Listen to the market, but do not lose your core values, which are the reason why they prefer you. Be creative and find solutions that are coherent with your philosophy.

HOTEL XCARET MÉXICO:
ALL VIEW, ALL SUITE & ALL FUN INCLUSIVE HOTEL

To tell you about our first hotel, I first need to tell you the story of how we got to this project. It all began in 1995, when we decided to buy a 444-acre land parcel adjacent to Xcaret park. We already knew then that the Group would grow and that, sooner or later, we would need our land reserves to be able to continue growing. From the beginning, we called it Destino Xcaret, since we realized that, in time, we would transform Xcaret into a destination itself. Although it is true that we did not clearly know what the final purpose of this land would be, we did know that we would do something special with it.

The idea behind Destino Xcaret was to gradually satisfy all the tourists' entertainment needs, from the moment they arrive at the destination to the moment they leave. In our ideal scenario, we would take care of our visitors from the moment they board a plane to come and visit us until the moment they return home. Our mission is to make our visitors have not just one of the best holidays of their lives—but the best!

#MUSTDO:

**If you know where you are going,
you will get there faster.**

Some years later, in 1999, a dispute arose with the owners of some neighboring lands, who claimed that our recently acquired plots belonged to them. In order to clear this up, a long legal process began. The proceedings lasted 11 years, but we were so convinced about the legality of our purchase that we never stopped our development on this land. In fact, Xplor park and Hotel Grand Flamenco are located precisely on these plots, and we never halted their construction, nor did we delay their opening, in spite of this dispute.

In the end, all was cleared up in the trial and the law confirmed our land ownership and rights we had always had over the property. It was a tedious process. The day it was all resolved, I remember feeling a weight being lifted off my shoulders, as if I had been reborn.

During this time, in 2002, as a result of my partner Marcos' negotiations with Grupo Occidental, we opened our 765 room Hotel Grand Flamenco. In this partnership, we put up the land and a percentage of money, and they contributed the rest of the capital needed. They were in charge of the hotel's operation and commercialization.

Initially, this hotel was conceived as part of Xcaret park; all guests arriving at the hotel were given access to the park.

However, our partners never understood the advantages of this product, and they didn't know how to commercialize it or maximize it. Finally, they unilaterally decided to stop offering the integrated package.

Destino Xcaret's land had a downside: it did not have a seafront, since that small strip of land was property of a family from Cozumel. After many years of talks and cajoling, in 2007 we finally succeeded in buying the piece of land that granted all our property full access to a beachfront. This was a strategic purchase for Destino Xcaret; it added profitability and value to all our land. Also, it offers spectacular views of Cozumel island, sitting on our beautiful Caribbean sea's horizon.

Architect Marcusi Constandse, would accompany his father to our board meetings ever since he was a child. Little by little, like a sponge, he absorbed the Group's culture and all the details of the management area his father was in charge of. In 2010, Marcusi presented a master plan for Destino Xcaret to the Board of Directors. In this plan, the partners needed to make a personal investment of the money needed to urbanize and create the infrastructure to start developing this property.

At first, this master plan had a definite patrimonial focus: the land was to be divided between partners so that, following specific building regulations, each family developed the projects they wanted on their own land. We adopted this proposal and got to work.

We began making arrangements to begin building the major works that would make up this master plan, like a 1.2 mile long river, including four small islands, five inlets with their five waterways connecting to the sea (this would give our property two seafront views), high quality roads, and all the necessary underground infrastructure for water, electricity, optic fiber, gas, and drainage.

Having formed our Trust at the end of 2010, and because of the Group's evolution, we realized that this project had huge potential and a vocation that should be integral to the Group, not just the individual partners. Due to this, in 2013, Marcusi presented us with a reconceptualized vision of Destino Xcaret, introducing a new plan, now in line with the Group's growth objectives.

«NOTHING IS MORE POWERFUL THAN AN IDEA WHOSE TIME HAS COME.»

VÍCTOR HUGO

The Constandses were originally in the hotel business, the founding partners of the Palace hotel chain many years ago. When Xcaret came into being, they stepped away from that world, but always remained nostalgic about going back to this sector. Personally, I always delayed this project, because in my view, we still had a lot to do in our parks. Besides, many other investors were building hotels, but not that many parks. However, over the past few years we have noticed that the tourists arriving at our destination are not only seeking sun and sea. People increasingly want to learn about our culture, they want to know about and interact with our people, and to xperience our traditions; they have been requesting activities to do during their visit other than going to the beach.

Many hotel owners had realized this too, and started offering visits to our parks and to archaeological sites as part of their guests' stay. Others have built small aquatic parks, skating rings, and even a circus show inside their facilities.

It was then that *we had an epiphany*: we already have the entertainment, and the parks, and the transportation, and the Mexican traditions, and the visits to archaeological sites. We have the perfect complement to a hotel! Why not, then, build a hotel and join the trend? Besides, we wanted tourists to have the best vacations in their lives, attending to them from the moment they arrived at the airport to the moment they went back home. So we decided to try our first hotel product in some lots adjacent to Xcaret we had acquired during the years. This way, we would see to our visitors during their entire stay, providing them with high quality services and unique and safe xperiences, as if a family member were attending to them. A full vacation xperience for the whole family.

The day had come: it was at this precise moment in the Group's history that three extraordinary concepts converged, when the hotel dreams of my partners, the parks xperience, and a new vacation club system coalesced. What a superb idea! Three important businesses were being born: a 5-star hotel with all its profits; that same hotel purchasing tickets to our parks and tours for all the hotel guests; and, finally, selling the hotel's singular vacation club to guests, a one-of-a-kind concept in the world: «all fun inclusive».

Marcusi presented a 15-year project divided in stages, including 5200 hotel rooms; a commercial complex called Pueblo del Río with entertainment and commercial areas along a 2-mile river; a Grand Convention Center; and a 12,000-seat auditorium. We realized that all we invested in this project would maximize the business units we already had, thus creating the necessary 1 + 1 = 3 synergy. We approved the concept, and all of us partners had to give back the land we had partitioned and divided among ourselves, reincorporating these pieces of land into the company and reintegrating them to the Group's Trust—which now included a hotel business with its own rules. Once again, we acted for the sake of the Group's good and made a necessary decision, the right decision for its future.

From 2014 to 2017, we undertook infrastructure work on rivers, coves, and the spiral pyramid. Marcusi Constandse, the Group's Vice Chair of Management and Finance, and David Quintana, Vice Chair of Strategy and Development, were the ones in charge of this impressive work: the former, of dealing with bureaucratic steps, finances, and of starting and running operations; the latter, as the architect leading the conceptualization, design, and construction of the project. Even before getting started, we engaged in conversations with EarthCheck to ensure we were working hand-in-hand, right from the start of the project. This later proved very rewarding when our hotel became the first in Latin America to be awarded EarthCheck's Planning and Design Certification.

As park-builders, we had some initial doubts about the hotel project—not about its functional, aesthetic, or construction specifications, but about who would be operating and commercializing it. It was our first hotel, we did not belong to any chain and, in our view, our xperience in this field was scant. The main national and international operators approached us with very tempting offers. Still, we—the partners—agreed that the best choice was to do it ourselves, so we decided to take a chance! We backed this idea up with our xperience and the quality of the service we offered in our parks, with the excellent results in our marketing area, and, above all, with the solidity and prestige of our brand: Xcaret.

The partners told me they were convinced we should operate two modalities: one, the all fun inclusive model, including unlimited admissions to our parks and tours, plus round-trip transportation between the airport and the hotel; the other, the traditional all-inclusive model, including only the room and the meals. I always pointed out that there were more than 500 luxury hotels in the destination similar to the latter model, and that we were the only ones who could offer the former model. We should take advantage of this opportunity to use this concept exclusively. It took us months to make this decision, but we finally started with one product, a single model. Today, we celebrate the fact that this is the concept that set us apart from all the rest. Now it is our main strength in the accommodation market. We succeeded in offering integrated, complete, super fun vacations—a winning combination.

This way, the price of the room includes visits to our parks and tours, operating as an extension of the hotel's garden. Basically, you can do all that you have the time to do: during the day, you can go to Xplor; at night, watch the Xcaret México Espectacular show; the following day, go to Xichén Itzá, perhaps have dinner in Xoximilco. The average length of the stay at the hotel is almost six days, and the guests get to visit between four to five parks—that is, one or two parks each day, except on the days they arrive and depart.

This is possible thanks to a comfortable and strategic transportation system. We have a shuttle with a defined route going around from one park to the next all day long, which facilitates planning your itinerary; it allows you to enjoy breakfast in peace at the hotel and visit the park you prefer any time you want. You do not have to get up at 5 a.m. to grab some food and be ready at the hotel entrance by 7 a.m., the time when our buses arrive at other hotels.

My son, David, and I designed the rooms with two rules in mind. Whereas traditional hotels have a limited number of suites—typically consisting of a bigger room with a separate living room, for a higher price, of course—we have chosen to offer only this type of room, with an integrated living-mini-dining room: an all-suite hotel. We also offer a view to the sea or the landscape from any point in the room—the bed, the washbasin, the jacuzzi, the shower, the toilet: an all-view hotel.

The decoration in the room, the tapestry, the tiles in the shower, are all inspired in the tree of life from our logo. The tiles, designed in-house, were hand-made in Yucatán over two years. Waste bins are traditional Mexican market bags. We also place a bromeliad in every room, taken from our greenhouse in Xcaret park. The hotel's Oriental restaurant is called Xin Gao, a Mexican play on words that might have its own Chinese explanation—*gau xing* means «happiness». The honey xampoo, besides being organic and scented with a characteristic fragrance from the region, is labelled with large print so that it is legible and no one has to wear their glasses.

One of the Group's precepts is that all that is printed, from the tickets to the menu, must be legible without having to wear glasses. The idea is that when you get to your room at night and you realize that you did not have to put on your glasses all day long, you say to yourself, «Even my eyesight improved at Xcaret, I never had to wear glasses.» Also, wherever possible, we have lowered the height of the steps in our staircases by one inch, so that, when going up the stairs, any guest feels somewhat different and can say, «I never felt better than at Xcaret, I didn't get tired when climbing stairs.»

Xcaret is a state of mind.

The only disagreement among partners about the room's design was the bathroom concept. One of them insisted that for reasons pertaining to hygiene, odor, humidity, and noise, it should always be contained within four walls. We insisted on changing this paradigm. One of the solutions was to enclose the toilet in a small room whose view to the room, through a special glass window, could be controlled by merely flicking a switch, allowing it to be either opaque or transparent. The rest of the bathroom opens to the room and to the view. Thanks to the vote of confidence by the partners, our rooms have some of the most xensual bathrooms I have seen anywhere.

#ENTREPTIP:

We must banish «it can't be done» from our vocabulary and replace it with «it can certainly be done». We can do difficult straight away; impossible takes us a little longer.

The rooms cost more than usual, of course, but our starting point was what we wanted the hotel to be like, not how much it should cost. To get where we wanted, we built four sample rooms in Xcaret park, where we did all our tests. We used to spend the night to see if it all worked well, and made the necessary adjustments during the day, until the rooms were just as they are in the hotel today.

As for recruiting human talent, we had to hire 1500 collaborators almost overnight. The human talent area requested that I buy buses to bring collaborators from Tulum and Cancún every day. I refused for several reasons: we already have buses driving back and forth in different shifts to bring colleagues who have no cars, but these vehicles coming from Cancún would only have time to make one trip coming in the morning and another one going back at night. Besides, collaborators would have to take a bus that would take 1 hour to get to our bus stop, and then spend another 1 ½ to get to the hotel to start their shifts. In total, they would spend 5 hours every day commuting between home and work—one third of their productive day spent on a bus. I found that outrageous! Consequently, my instruction was categorical: look only for local collabaorators. I can proudly say that we received fifteen thousand applications for our 1500 positions. There are a lot of people from other companies who want to come work for us because they know about our work philosophy, about who we are and where we are going. People are the soul of our company, we treasure them.

For the executive team, we had to find the best professionals in the field, which proved to be difficult. At the beginning of 2016, we hired a team of hotel experts we could consult with about the management of our future first hotel. However, we forgot to consider that as park-builders, we had a completely different idea to those held in the traditional hotel business, and that in this business, some professionals have big egos. We let them do what they were best at and agreed to their conditions. They started the project miles away from the Group's concept, and a similar type of rivalry as first xperienced between Xcaret and Xel-Há emerged once again.

We had a very hard time adapting. There were several highs and lows, particularly as the new team assimilated our culture and DNA. As a consequence of this process, the appointed executive director and most of his people, not being able to integrate to our team, had to leave the company by mid-2017. I clearly remember that by then we were finishing the construction and equipment of our first hotel adventure, and that only four months away from inauguration day, reservations added up to merely 3% occupancy for the winter season—the high season for tourism.

Something was really wrong, we had to take action. We immediately brought aboard a vastly xperienced hotelier, who also shared with us fundamental concepts: our deep love for Mexico, innovation, sustainability, and, above all, our passion for becoming part of this project and collaborating with the team.

Luckily, in less than a year they have realized that using the parks' culture and infrastructure to their best advantage is quite profitable. Likewise, the park team has learned to work collaboratively with the hotel, recognizing the added value it has given to the Group, as a new business unit with which more can be accomplished. In fact, our present goal is to achieve the hotel's complete integration and alignment to the Group's precepts, ethics, and philosophy.

Before beginning operations, we wanted to make sure our staff was prepared and ready for the adventure. To accomplish this, we trained by having our friends and family members over for what hoteliers call a «soft opening». In November 2017, my family organized a «Quintanada», a gathering of the extended Quintana family. We invited around 500 people and hosted them at the hotel as our first guests. This way, we could fine-tune details and correct mistakes detected during this big rehearsal.

On December 1st, 2017, with a big downpour and a rainbow—in Hawaii, having rain during a special event is a sign of good fortune—we opened Hotel Xcaret México, the first all fun inclusive hotel. By January 2018, a month after its opening, we had an 80% occupancy rate, and we finished the year up four percentage points. This, I am told, is an xtraordinary thing in the hotel industry, which made us very happy indeed. The second year closed at a similar occupancy rate, although at a price that was 50% higher than the previous year. This being the first hotel operation we have handled ourselves, I deem it a complete success.

Hotel Xcaret México is a product that has passed its litmus test, although we cannot rest on our laurels. Now, it is time to learn, to work on the details and services, and to apply the knowledge we have acquired, fostering our continuous improvement. We can rely on our xperience of xcellence in service and quality, the uniqueness of our product, and on organic marketing and commercialization—by word-of-mouth—as well as an unparalleled digital strategy; we are putting all this to good use in our hotels.

«THE RACE FOR QUALITY HAS NO FINISH LINE.»

ANONYMOUS

To continue with the second phase of our Destino Xcaret master plan, in January 2019, we began the building work on the second hotel development, Hotel Xcaret Arte, following the same concept, but with some improvements and focusing on adults and more conventions. Each one of its five houses or buildings represents a specific branch of the national arts: painters, actors, singers, poets, and artisans. We have also started a third boutique hotel next to the beach, with only 63-rooms, each with its own swimming pool and a miniature jellyfish aquarium. To help speed up these projects, the partners have agreed to reinvest half of the Group's profits on hotels. Of course, at the same time, we are taking steps to get bank loans, putting our hotels up as collateral—never our parks, as our patrimonial trust forbids it.

#ENTREPTIP:

Things must be done right from the start. You'll never get a second chance to make a good first impression. Excellence must be part of our routine.

VACATION CLUB

In the 1950's, a movement grew out of the desire to share quality time with family and friends. Families, especially, aspired to having a holiday home in a beautiful setting, like a beach, a mountain, an island, or some other tropical paradise, depending on their favorite sports and the time of the year. At first, some visionaries built condominiums where families could share a property, purchasing the use of one or two weeks per year for a number of years—the famous *timeshares*. Weeks were sold as fixed units and on fixed dates. Later, in response to customer demand, a system of rotating accommodation was created, allowing the commercialization of condos by season and by type of unit—*season membership* and *floating units.*

In the 1970's, the *vacation exchange* program came into being, in which a condominium or villa could be swapped, so a family could travel to other destinations, while other families could visit one's own. Years later, the traditional hotel business changed to the *all-inclusive* concept and the *all-inclusive membership.* Families paid an annual membership fee, which tended to increase, to be able to keep their vacation property in optimal conditions—plus an additional fee for food and beverages. Nowadays, the *vacation club* concept includes more benefits: members can get discounted fees from suppliers of holiday services, including resort and hotel stays, flights, cruises, yachts, luxury house and condo rentals, car rentals, park admissions, tours, and golf courses, among others.

In the future, loyalty programs and technology will play a major role, as we can learn about our customers' preferences from their history and online searches. Soon, digital platforms will offer membership schemes specifically tailored to suit customers' lifestyle and needs, considerably reducing commercialization costs. This will apply not only to hotel memberships, but to cruises and, soon enough, even trips to the moon!

Around the time we opened Hotel Xcaret México, we developed a new vacation club for the hotel with a differentiated model. It is not a conventional timeshare. It operates as a discount club, where members register under different membership types and categories to get up to 25% discount on our hotel, plus other very worthwhile discounts and added values within our parks, among others. This is a unique business model under the *all fun inclusive* banner. Its objective is to attract future customers to our hotels and parks by nurturing loyal, happy members and return customers. And, of course, our product complies with our philosophy and our sustainability model.

Today, this club is a reality. We have broken paradigms and surpassed the main indicators in the vacation club industry.

XAVAGE

As I have said before, an important point for us, right from the beginning, has been increasing our capacity. Xcaret is the biggest park, able to hold twelve thousand people every day. In Xel-Há, we have capacity for six thousand, a number we could increase, because many more people can swim in the cove—it is really a matter of extending our restaurants and bathrooms. However, in a park like Xplor, which includes zip-lines, our growth capacity is limited, since even with four zip-lines per tower, it takes more than an hour for one person to finish the whole course.

We decided that our next park, Xavage, would also be an adventure park, but now including six different attractions, each with at least four tracks. I have already talked about the zip-line emulating the flight of a hawk. Now, in Xavage, visitors take off from a double-height platform, so they fly twice as long and twice as far. Our parks complement each other, otherwise, they would be competing against and cannibalizing each other.

The most visited tourist attraction in New Zealand is the Shotover River, a fast 12-seater jet boat that travels along a narrow river at full speed, grazing the walls of cliffs and doing 360-degree turns wherever the river is wide enough to allow it. A pure adrenaline rush! We wanted to do the same in our Xoximilco lands. We widened the canal, which we had originally dredged at sea level, to be able to navigate it on fast jet boats for several miles. We have designed a closed continuous course, where jet boats leave the pier at intervals of only a few minutes.

We also created *rock climbers*, tubular all-terrain vehicles with huge tires, which are driven along a pre-determined circuit and are able to climb over obstacles and rocks without ever flipping over. We build these vehicles ourselves for the four tracks in Xavage. Before doing so, we procured many vehicles of this sort, all from different brands, we pulled them apart, studied them, and identified what the best feature in each one was. The idea was to find one we could use as it was and adapt it, but none of them measured up. There are similar vehicles in the market, but ours needed special characteristics, particularly power and safety. Our Dreamers are not car engine or suspension specialists. Still, they were able to assemble the parts that helped them get what we wanted. *Practice makes perfect.* All vehicles were ready two years before the park's inauguration. We produced and are still producing two per month.

As I have said before, in Cancún and the Riviera Maya most rivers are underground, at sea level. To have «white-water rapids», to offer the xperience of a bumpy and splashy ride, we had to build a river that begins its course some 40 feet above sea level and runs for almost a mile. This is the longest man-made white-water river ever built. (My grand-mother would have said: «Why so many bumps, with such an even road?») A similar course to this one—but short-er—was built for the kayak competition in the 2012 London Olympics. Without the necessary slope, we had to create the current and turbulence in our river by employing five immense 500-horsepower turbines. *That is quite a large herd of horses!*

To develop all these technologies, our team of Dreamers make dreams come true. Ideas normally originate in-house, they are discussed, and those ingenious colleagues get to work building the prototypes. We are lucky to have in our team some exceptionally clever and very creative people, jacks of all trades who design, build models and improve prototypes, until they become what we originally imag-ined, what we need them to be. *A good rooster can crow anywhere.*

ALL THE CREDENTIALS

Throughout the year, we evaluate and validate our perfor-mance with the help of certifications based on national and international standards. These certifications allow us to pursue continuous improvements and xcellence. Our best practices have resulted in awards and certifications that recognize our efforts in terms of quality of service, hygiene, marketing, security, sustainability, and technology, among others. Among the most salient awards are:

- Sectur's distinction marks: M for being a model company, H for hygiene, S for best environmental practices
- EarthCheck Sustainability Certification given to our parks
- EarthCheck Planning and Designing given to Hotel Xcaret México and to Destino Xcaret
- Certification for Quality and Security Standards by Thomas Cook (CGS)
- Certification for complying with security and services requirements by the Association for Challenge Course Technology
- Cristal International Certification given to our parks and Hotel Xcaret México for health, hygiene, and security
- «Cero Rezago Educativo» («No Educational Lag») distinction from INEA
- Socially Responsible Enterprise, CEMEFI—the first ones in the tourist sector and awarded to us every year since 2002
- 2013 Guinness Record recognition for the greatest number of macaws born in a year: 132 specimens
- ALPZA (Asociación Latinoamericana de Parques, Zoológicos y Acuarios) Certification for complying with operation standards

- AZCARM (Asociación de Zoológicos, Criaderos y Acuarios de México) Accreditation for complying with the highest Mexican operation standards
- TripAdvisor Certificate of Excellence for all our xperiences

Among our awards and recognitions, the following are note-worthy:

- Best Companies to Work in Mexico (since 2005) by Great Place to Work Institute
- Best practices in social responsibility, awarded 15 times by CEMEFI
- Enterprise with Green Innovation by OECD
- Sustainable Tourism Prize by SKÅL
- Tourism for Tomorrow award by the World Travel and Tourism Council
- One in 100 most innovating enterprises in Mexico by Mundo Ejecutivo
- Best Mexican Companies by ITESM, Deloitte, and CitiBanamex
- Best managed affiliated program in Latin America, granted on four occasions by PerformanceIN
- Heel Prize to Market Excellence by the Meeting Professionals International Mexico
- Brass Ring Awards for our excellence in marketing, Brass Ring Award for Public Relations campaigns on two occasions, granted by the IAAPA
- Best Video in Latin America award in the «Picture This Festival» competition by Sony Picture's Planeta

- Macaws documentary, winner of Best Video most voted by viewers, Best Video in the small companies' category, and Best video in all categories, in the Boston College's Corporate Citizenship Film Festival
- Best tourism site, twice granted by Expansión
- Best tour reservation platform provider by Viator
- UN Global Compact members: Founders and members of the Board for the Mexican Network
- Ethics and Values Award granted by the Confederation of Industrial Chambers of Mexico

XCARET

- Best international park and Best aquatic park outside the U.S. by Travvy Awards
- Ulysses Prize for Excellence and Innovation granted by the World Tourism Organization: the first Mexicans to attain it
- Liseberg Applause Award for the Best Park in the World (2018) by the IAAPA; it is considered the «Oscar» of the amusement parks in the world.

XEL-HÁ:

- One of the 13 Wonders in Mexico (2007)

XPLOR:

- PR News Product Launch for the public relations campaign for Xplor's launch

XENSES:

- Best Traveling digital campaign by Web Marketing

HOTEL XCARET MÉXICO:

- Family Getaway and Reader's Choice by Travel & Leisure.
- World's Greatest Places by Time
- Prevue Visionary Gold Award to the Best Cultural Immersion Experience
- Silver for the Best All Inclusive Resort
- Best Tourism and Hospitality Work Prize to Innovation and Technology and People's Choice Award by Obras magazine
- The most searched hotel by Hotels.com
- Golden Apple Hotels

I have a great team of collaborators; I owe to them several of the recognitions I've received along my career.

- Businessman of the year (2004) granted by Asociación Mexicana de Mujeres Empresarias Riviera Maya.
- Prize «Antonio Enriquez Savignac» (2011) for Touristic Merit
- Prize for Touristic leadership granted by the Consejo Nacional de Empresarios Turísticos (CNET) (2012)
- Prize for Touristic Business Merit granted by CONCANACO and presented by the President of Mexico (2013)

- «Llave del Progreso» Prize granted by AMAIT a symbol of commitment, dedication and love for Mexico (2017)
- The Most Trusted CEO by Great Place to Work Institute (2018)
- Lifetime Achievement Award by the Latin American Hotel Investment Community (2019)
- Citizen of the year by Fundación Azteca (2019)
- AMAV Recognition to Touristic Trajectory by the Asociación Mexicana de Agencias de Viajes de Quintana Roo (2019)

However, for me, a job well done is its own reward. These recognitions and certifications encourage us to keep dreaming with our feet on the ground.

LEARNING FROM THE PANDEMIC
THE MOST SEVERE CRISIS
IN OUR LIFETIME
CHAPTER 12

In one way or another, the COVID-19 pandemic has affected every human being on the planet—a truly undeclared world war. It has killed hundreds of thousands of people, and led to the bankruptcy of thousands of companies— from family businesses to multinational enterprises, banks, airlines, factories— and even entire countries. It has left millions of people jobless. It made us understand that the virus does not discriminate between class, gender, age, ethnicity or political affiliation—though sadly socioeconomic background does determine the way it is experienced.

For the planet this crisis has been like a magnitude 10 earthquake, something we couldn't even imagine might happen. Today we know it could have been worse. We still have a lot more to learn about the virus, but what I do know is that it is very important to capitalize on this unfortunate experience that paralyzed the world for more than a year, leaving lasting scars.

The world has had to respond immediately as a whole, as inhabitants of the same planet coming together and learning each day how to behave for the next day. We experienced days of continuous adjustment, days of solidarity, days of helping each other. The priority was to slow down the contagion, to gain time while learning how to tackle the virus more efficiently until we found a vaccine that would protect us from it. The immediate solution was to stay at home, comply with social distancing measures and adapt to the mandatory use of face masks outside our homes whenever we were likely to meet more people. When my great-grandchildren ask me why, in 2020, I did not carry out any projects, I will have to tell them it was because I spent my time washing my hands.

We realized how fragile human beings are as part of a wider ecosystem. The pandemic made us conscious that if we wanted to keep living on this planet, we would have to comprehend its vulnerability and work towards stopping its deterioration, which is also our deterioration. There were two things we were certain of: that the road to recovery would be long, but also that it would eventually come to an end.

Many of us lost loved ones. Countless people found themselves without their daily routine and sources of income. Many others lost their businesses. We had time to think and not to think, time to find ourselves and focus only on our breathing, to empty our minds, to meditate and nurture our inner world.

It is at the hardest times when our true self comes out. Those are the moments of truth, and sometimes truth it is not what we would expect it to be. In crises like this one, it is important to think ahead and decide how we are going to face the new reality, whatever it is and however it comes. For this, we need a lot of each of the following ingredients: a positive attitude, determination, integrity, tolerance, generosity, solidarity, communication, humility, joy and love.

In the course of these days, there were two critical moments that involved hours of walking around my desk thinking about what to do, waking up in the middle of the night with another hopefully better solution, whole days spent reading everything I could about COVID-19 and its possible consequences. The first of these was the decision to close our parks, the hotel, and the building works in progress. The second was deciding when and how to reopen.

BRINGING DOWN THE CURTAIN

Besides being important to the local tourism industry and generating a strong economic spill in the region, Grupo Xcaret has been a local model because of its social responsibility and leadership in matters such as resilience, creative uses of technology, strategic marketing, and unique products that help protect our environment. We are the point of reference in the area for the daily dollar exchange rate. We have set the example of having clean, well-maintained public bathrooms. We have pioneered good practices in tourism and environmental matters that many seek to follow. We are, in brief, the embodiment of fun, quality and safety in the region. Because of that, when faced with delicate situations of vulnerability and emergency, we feel compelled to set the best example so that together we can solve problems effectively and get back on our feet as soon as possible.

Deciding a closing date was one of the most difficult and distressing decisions. The hotel and parks had a good occupancy rate at that time. We could have waited another week, but seeing the pandemic was spreading so fast we decided to close immediately to protect our collaborators and our guests. Someone with a good standing in the community had to take responsibility and set the example, so that is what we did: three days before the weekend we announced that Sunday, March 22, would be the last day that we would remain open. The wide dissemination of our message led many of the local tourism businesses to follow suit and refrain from taking any health risks, speeding up their own closure plans.

Closure meant sending home 8 000 collaborators and 4 500 construction workers—450 temporary workers had just been hired for the Easter Break high-season, the rest of them were on a permanent basis—without being able to tell them how long this would last. Despite the distress caused by the health contingency, all members of our team were at ease because they knew they were part of our Xcaret Family. We have always made it through difficult times together, in which we all look after one another and are willing to sacrifice part of our time and income for the sake of all.

We reached an agreement with them to split the quarantine period in two phases: the critical phase, during which the parks and hotel would be completely closed, and which in the end lasted for three months; and the restart phase, estimated to last for up to 6 months until reaching the break-even point, perhaps close to Christmas. We agreed a salary for each one of these two phases. Once back in the black, I believe it will take us about a year to regain our pace and to generate profits, and another year to cover the debt generated by this pandemic.

Since the closing date, we have produced and circulated a daily comparative report with the number of new COVID-19 cases and deaths in Quintana Roo, in Mexico and in other countries. This has offered us a reference to measure ourselves against, and helped us to visualize the development of the pandemic in our region. The objective was to focus on our reality within this contingency to be able to take responsible decisions on when and how to proceed.

One of the secrets to overcome any crisis is to learn, learn, learn, but also to communicate, communicate, communicate—communicate to your business partners, collaborators, banks, customers, suppliers, and to local, national and even international stakeholders. Offering timely and accurate information gives everyone the confidence that will underpin a good outcome.

It was, on one hand, a very difficult and expensive decision. On the other, it was consistent with my main priority, which underpins our company's philosophy: in making any decision, people's xafety takes precedence over everything else. It was a matter of values, of corporate culture, in which the lives and well-being of people—our staff and their families, our visitors, the wider community—are far more important than the company's profitability.

LIFE MUST GO ON

Setting the reopening date was the other most difficult and stressful decision. On April 22—almost five weeks after the closure of all our tourism companies—based on the results of our daily reports, in accordance with national, state-level and municipal health officials, and after complying with all the appropriate qualifications and certifications, we decided to announce June 1st as a tentative reopening date for our Xcaret Mexico Hotel and Xcaret Park. In the end, the authorities urged us, as a precaution, to delay our reopening, so we reopened on June 15. The remaining parks did so on July 1.

To get Cancun and the Riviera Maya up-and-running again was going to be a complicated and slow process. New outbreaks would be a certainty while there was no vaccine. We knew visitors would not show up until they felt that all health and safety measures were covered, but we also knew that as long as we did not officially open the destination, no travel operators would send tourists our way, and no airline would bring them to us. What came first, the chicken or the egg? We also knew that in June and July it would cost us more to be open than closed, because during the reopening phase the occupancy rate would not exceed 30%.

It was important that we signaled that Cancún and the Riviera Maya were open for business and that they were safe to visit. Gradually, other businesses would restart as soon as they were able to. Having kept the pandemic at bay, the region—that had been on the brink of a social crisis during the lockdown—could once again flourish.

#MUSTDO:
Ethics must always take precedence over efficiency, principles over results, people over things

Saying that if we opened our businesses the risk of outbreaks would increase, or that if we did not open them our collaborators would be left without a job, is a false dichotomy. There are thousands of possibilities in between these two extremes, and we must find the best ones to succeed in the best possible manner. If we prioritized profits over people's health, we would soon be left without collaborators, without customers, and therefore without a company to run. But if we prioritized the health of our coworkers and customers, the health of the company would recover soon.

When reopening, as an important measure to ensure xafety and build trust, we made over 8,000 rapid tests available to our collaborators over a couple of weeks. The tests helped us detect individuals who tested positive for COVID-19, and also helped us identify others who had already had the virus, so were already carriers of antibodies and very possibly immune to it. All those who tested positive were subjected to additional PCR tests in a private laboratory, and of all the positive rapid tests only 4 came back as negative.

We also contributed to the creation of reopening guidelines for members of the International Association of Amusement Parks and Attractions (IAAPA) and the World Tourism Organization (WTO). With what we learned in these processes, and with our own knowledge, we created a detailed protocol for the reopening—Xafety 360°—soon adopted by the World Travel and Tourism Council (WTTC) and Mexico's Ministry of Tourism. Finally, we uploaded both the full protocol document and the summarized guidance onto our website, making it freely accessible to whoever needed it. In moments like this, the best thing we can do is to share what we know. It is about working together to move on sooner.

The business world must not seek progress by opposing one thing to another, but must instead move ahead by reconciling them. Running a company is never easy, but it is always exciting: it is the art of reconciling opposite realities that sometimes appear irreconcilable, so that people always win.

Taking stock of our experience, we know that the biggest obstacle during this crisis was fear—a fear that was real and justified as well as being the product of current forms of communication, in which we were both actors and victims of this gigantic drama. There was an overload of news—a mix of ignorance, disinformation, sensationalism and fake news, passed on as in a game of Chinese whispers—amplified ex-

ponentially through the smart phone and social media, creating an environment of exaggeration and alarmism that generated distrust and fear.

AN UNCERTAIN FUTURE

From now on, everything that was once fixed will become
variable. In times of crisis, we must stop thinking about most
of our expenses as fixed—from our salaries and the cost of
our rent and our insurance, to our supplies—whether the crisis is economic, cybernetic, or related to work, health or the
environment.

In the future, all our facilities will have some important
changes: ceilings will be higher, we will have to section many
public spaces, we will try to avoid enclosed areas, and we
will enlarge common areas and widen corridors. We will use
new materials, preferably with surfaces that are non-porous,
so more hygienic and easy to clean, such as ceramic tiles,
glass, acrylic paint, and stainless steel coverings and accessories.

We will avoid or reduce the use of restroom accessories,
such as door handles, handrails, elevator buttons, water and
coffee dispensers, and other objects requiring people to
touch surfaces that everyone else touches. This will be achieved with electronic sensors or foot pedals.

We will protect our dining and buffet areas from airborne
droplets and particles, and from contact with guests' hands,
with the help of a single designated member of staff serving
from the inside. Or we can offer an a la carte service with QR
code menus or our guests can rely on large sign boards, por-
table blackboards, or the memory of our waiters as they reel
off the day's dishes.

In terms of business, I realized that this is a great opportunity to reinforce the model of direct sales through digital

channels so that customers are no longer in direct contact with a cashier or seller, avoiding the need for an exchange of money or for the physical use of credit cards. This is where Hotel Xcaret México's «All Fun Inclusive» model fits perfectly: with a simple transaction, from the comfort of their own electronic device, guests can purchase a package that includes transportation on arrival and departure, accommodation, food and beverages and all the fun needed for their whole stay—all this within the strictest quality, xafety and hygiene protocols. What more can anyone ask for?

The great challenge now will be to ensure that social distance does not become emotional distance, the opposite of the face-to-face contact that we need to build—a more inclusive and humane world for all. The direct contact and engagement between owners, executives, staff and customers, which was already a feature of the business landscape, is an imperative in the «new normal»—our new reality. There is a new awareness that has made us increasingly sensitive to the need to seek more direct interactions, and more personal and warm relationships to strengthen us all.

We urgently need to change our lifestyle to a more sustainable way of living; we have to think globally and consume locally; we have to reduce, reuse, and recycle; we have to adopt clean energy, be more efficient in our use of resources, reduce our carbon footprint, avoid polluting, make better use of water, and generate less waste. We have to live closer to work and to our children's school—safety will always be closer to home. We don't need much to have good lives.

In a crisis, my advice is that you put an immediate break on your investments and projects to rearrange your priorities—both your personal ones and your financial ones. Take care of the small expenses—a little hole can sink a big boat. Until you know how long the situation is going to last, and, when you are likely to start generating profits again, be mindful of your resources so that you can cope with the worst-case scenario. A critical situation could last longer than we can stay solvent. We know that difficult times pass, but people with fortitude and determination remain, so be strong and take care of your cash to stay afloat until the storm goes away.

A useful approach I have learned over time is that, in any crisis, you first have to consider the worst-case scenario and propose solutions for it. Anything that happens thereafter will be a bonus. Proper insurance, for example, is not a luxury anymore but a must, and if you do not have one it is important to have a contingency fund or an authorized credit line, or a combination of all these.

#MUSTDO:

**Cash flow and preparation
are the lifesavers in any crisis.**

I don't think the world has changed too much with the pandemic, apart from the very sad fact that we lost so many loved ones, and from the disastrous economic and social consequences. However, what I do think has changed, without a doubt, is the way we see the world and our lives: the pandemic made us more aware of the meaning of our passage through life, making us more human, supportive, and more sensitive to our environment. I am confident that it made us better people. The most beautiful thing in life is love—allow yourself to love and to be loved.

We have lived through the worst disaster of our times, but luckily 99.99% of humans are still here, alive and kicking. There is so much to be grateful for! Personally, I have learned many valuable lessons. I learned not to take things for granted, that life is not a given, and that we have to be ready for any contingency. Above all, we must all learn to let go. This is the world and this the moment we have to live in, so we must accept it with serenity, wisdom and joy. We must seek for happiness because there is nothing else. Life is short and can change in the blink of an eye, so never stop dreaming and never stop making your dreams a reality. Live, enjoy life and always pursue your dreams.

COMING SOON...

WHAT
COMES NEXT...

CHAPTER 13

XIBALBÁ

Currently, we are working on the construction of new parks, both in Quintana Roo and in Yucatán. We are conducting studies to build a big natural park in the western region of the state of Yucatán, because we are convinced that we need to develop and set off new tourist hubs.

We are betting on the state of Yucatán as the future of tourism in the peninsula because, unlike Quintana Roo, Yucatán has cathedrals, convents and monasteries, colonial cities, big caverns, xenotes 60 feet underground, henequen haciendas, and much more. Except for Tulum's archaeological site and Xel-Há's cove, we have developed the main attractions in Cancún and the Riviera Maya. In Yucatán, the attractions are already there. We only need to invest in infrastructure, design tours, extend the roads, build more hotels in different and new tourist hubs, and advertise. Although the number of visitors may be smaller, Yucatán has the vocation and the potential to become the second most important tourist destination in the country.

Near Valladolid, since 2014, we have been working underground developing a new and important park. It will include nine big xenotes 550 yards apart from each other, forming a huge circle. They will be connected by long canyons, rivers, tunnels and caverns. Its name will be Xibalbá, the Maya underworld.

We will conclude this magnificent work in December 2021, so it is rather urgent that we plan ahead for the next project requiring the heavy machinery that will become available when we finish this park.

GREAT LITTLE HOTELS

I have three vices or hobbies: xenotes, belts, and shoes. If you walked into my wardrobe, you would laugh at seeing almost only moccasins and top siders, all in some shade of brown, but all brown, nonetheless. As for the first of these vices, I always say that they are like women: there is no ugly xenote.

Over the past 15 years, I have «collected» a series of incredible xenotes—some full of stalactites and stalagmites, others with turquoise-blue or emerald-green waters, gigantic or tiny, open and lush with vegetation or enclosed, with the midday rays of sun filtering through a miniature hole in the ceiling of the cavern. My passion has been to fit them out so they can be used for tourism.

In the state of Yucatán, there is an inventory of more than 10,000 xenotes. For the fifty I have been fortunate enough to acquire, I had to explore at least 500. Half of them open to the sky, and the other half are still enclosed. My team of xenote xplorers is made up of four to six people: half of them enter the caverns with me, the other half provide support from outside. We go in pairs, never alone. We are assisted by squads of eight strong local farmers, who use pulleys, set up on a tripod made with logs, to lower us into and pull us out of the caves. The mandatory equipment for those of us descending into the caves includes a harness—in the early days, we would use a rope tied to a wooden branch—, a life jacket, water shoes, a helmet, a waterproof floating lantern, and a pocket laser distance measurer.

In Yucatán's xenotes, there are at least 60 ft between the ground and the water below, which can range in depth between 2 feet and 262 feet. Since I am in charge of the exploration, it is my responsibility to descend first, notwithstanding the risks involved.

Most of these xenotes had never been explored before, no human had ever been inside them. When the water in the xenote was not very deep, we could see its history at the bottom: from modern plastic buckets to pre-Hispanic vestiges of clay pots, from the remains of animal bones to the skeletons of humans that may have fallen in and were never able to get out. There are thousands of years of history—maybe even millions, if we consider the development of its geological formations.

There were incidents that we did not pay much heed to when they happened, but that are now reflected in our procedure manual. Once, as I was beginning to descend, hanging about 13 feet below the ground surface, I started shouting, «Pull me up, pull me up, pull me up!» The team immediately pulled me up while I was swatting all around me, even at my face. During my half-darkened descent, I had upset a wasp's nest, who had decided to get even with me. The speedy rescue and my agile slaps stopped it from getting out of hand: only three stings above the nose and some very swollen cheeks from all the swatting. From that moment on, we learned to introduce a torch through the xenote's mouth a few minutes before going in to scatter any bee or wasp community awaiting for us.

Another time, I was uneventfully lowered into the xenote, and reached the water. I shone my light all around to scout the place and found a rock on an edge from which to hold on. I shouted to the people above, «Everything's OK!» and I unclipped from the rope. Next, they lowered my partner, for safety reasons. I remember swimming to that rock on the edge very slowly. I was tired and when I finally got to it, I could rest. My partner came down, then unclipped from the rope and swam towards me. Once he reached me, I told him I felt tired. He said he was too, and that he also had a headache. It did not take me long realize what was happening to us: there was not enough oxygen. The mouth of the xenote was so narrow that oxygen was not being renewed inside the cavern. Without thinking twice, we left that place immediately. We had been in real danger of asphyxiating; next, we would've fallen asleep in there, without realizing it. Once outside, I recovered quickly, but my partner was left with a headache that lasted all day. Since that day, we have never descended without a gadget that sets off an alarm if oxygen levels are too low.

Early on in these adventures, I remember arriving at a place from where we would descend into a cave. The 8-man squad in charge of the tripod and pulley had everything set up since early in the morning, but my partners, the xenote-finders, had forgotten to bring single climbing rope, the special type used when descending into or ascending out of water or a mountain. In our frustration, we could think of nothing but going to the hardware store in the nearest town and buying rope, the one everyone uses—the yellow double-braid nylon kind: a 238 feet roll. We went back to the place, cut the length needed, and passed it through the pulleys. All was ready, it was time to get started.

I fastened myself to the rope and was lowered, little by little. I noticed that, while descending, I was twirling slowly, and as I went further down the twirling got faster. I was probably two thirds of the way down when the ropes passing through the pulleys became twisted and got stuck, while I continued spinning faster and faster. We had not taken into account that the new rope was a triple braided rope, and that the threads were becoming unbraided, causing me to spin non-stop, and causing the ropes to become stuck in the pulleys. The men could not pull me up or lower me down. I was afraid of getting too dizzy and becoming unconscious. Luckily, my body withstood the hour I kept on spinning.

I do not know how they did it, but my companions eventually managed to disassemble the pulley and, with the help of some reinforcements they recruited, using sheer brute strength, they managed to pull up the tangle of ropes from which I was still dangling. The lesson we learned was that we must never improvise when it comes to security measures, you cannot afford to make things up as you go along. Human life cannot be put at risk because we only have one. Our body, if well treated, can remain healthy all our lives.

Nowadays, layovers in the state of Yucatán tend to happen in Mérida. Tourists go to Uxmal, and on the way back stop in the state capital; they travel to Valladolid, or Celestún to see the flamingos, and then go back for a layover in Mérida. We are hopeful the government will soon build a highway from Chichén Itzá to Uxmal, to close the circle. This will make it possible to travel through the whole state efficiently and will encourage investment in hotel chains along these routes, activating new tourist hubs. This is a medium-term project, but part of our mission is to provide support to this region's development now, exploiting its potential. Someone has to get that ball rolling. The state of Yucatán has a tourist vocation and we will help propel it. Remember that Cancún was not developed in one day.

For seven years, we have been doing hand tooled construction work on four iconic little boutique hotels. Their rooms are being built around four beautiful xenotes near the city of Valladolid, in Yucatán. Each hotel has 33 rooms, and all of them face the xenote. They each have three restaurants—one for each meal of the day—, a library, a game room, meditation caves, a chapel, and a xpa located in several caverns.

In one of the hotels, called «Laberinto de las Golondrinas»—Swallows' Labyrinth—two suites are sculpted from inside the rock itself. In another, the xpa is alongside a closed-in xenote. The third one is on the site of a henequen hacienda.

The commercial concept for these hotels is to be able to sell a tour of six to eight nights, two per hotel. The first day, you arrive around midday, you have lunch, you spend the rest of the afternoon enjoying the facilities at your leisure, and you dine. The following day, after breakfast, you go for a morning outing. When you return, same as the day before, you have lunch, enjoy the hotel, the xenote, and have dinner. On the third day, while you're out on your morning outing, we just pack up your wardrobe and transport it to the next hotel in your tour. Back from your outing, you will make your way to this second hotel, to the same room number, that you can open with your same key, and where you will find your wardrobe with all your belongings arranged just so. For the duration of your visit, you enjoy more of the same, getting to stay in these three or four little hotels throughout your stay. It is like going on a cruise, except by land—but boy-oh-boy, what a cruise ship!

NEW MEANS OF TRANSPORTATION

We have always had a small share of the cruise ship tourists arriving on Cozumel island: more than four million per year. Since this island is a long distance from the mainland, our park and tour sales to the cruise ships only amount to 3% of the Group's annual sales. Visitors arriving on these gigantic ships have to disembark, take a small boat to the pier, from there get on a tender to Playa del Carmen and, finally, take another vehicle to get to our parks.

To save them the time and to make it easy for them to reach us, we will bring them to our parks and tours directly from the cruise ships docked at Cozumel in two new tenders we recently acquired. These are powered catamaran boats with a cabin seating 600 passengers each. The challenge now is to see where they will dock—perhaps at a provisional pier, or at some other point near Xcaret we have yet to think of.

The idea is to improve the service they are receiving now and to make it easier, therefore increasing the number of visitors from the cruise ships to our parks and tours. By simplifying the logistics of their transfers, we can make sure that tourists have more time to enjoy themselves.

MY DREAM (MI XUEÑO)

Somebody has to make the first move, somebody has to be the scout, the trailblazer, the innovator who shows the mid-sized hotel chains that there are markets they have neglected. Both in the south of Quintana Roo and in the whole state of Yucatán, we lack hotels at the right distance from each other within a tourist route or tour.

My dream is that when we decide to journey through one of these states, we can travel at ease, knowing that at the end of the day we'll arrive at another hotel—part of the same chain— and find the same quality and service, a clean and safe hotel. That we only have to make a single reservation for all the layovers in the different places with the same hotel chain: one single service, different xperiences. Who knows, beyond just selling accommodation, we might end up selling the whole vacation package—the complete tour, including transportation. Awesome!

I want you to get caught in my dream. Create your own hotel: on a treetop, on a motor RV camper, on a glamping site, in floating rooms on a river or a lake, or in a farm—where the first thing you do when you wake up is pick your own oranges for your juice, or collect a few freshly laid eggs for breakfast, or bake your own bread. Build a thematic hotel, such as an hacienda surrounding a xenote, with a view of a natural area with flamingos or of an archaeological site. Just imagine your customer saying: «I stayed at an hacienda», «I slept in a xenote», or «I woke up with flamingos!»

In my opinion, these hotels should have 80, 120, or even 160 rooms and be modular, so that they can gradually expand. There should be enough distance between them so that the route from one to the next includes plenty of tourist attractions to occupy visitors all day in a fun and cultural way, including the hotel as part of the fun, without having to spend more. They would have to be located in the countryside or in small towns, that's why they should try to harmonize with the environment, in keeping with the region's own local vernacular architecture, preferably using local materials, and below three stories high. As opposed to conventional business hotels, the hotels' swimming pools should be generous in size, so that after a hot day's journey, the whole family can take their usual dip in the pool. Also, this hotel should include a good breakfast buffet, and the same for dinner.

My advice: dream and make it come true!

The longest walk begins with the first step; all your wisdom serves no purpose if you do not put it to good use. Our success lies in our being able to visualize our ideas in action, assess the risk, make the decision, and get on with it! A genius might start great projects, but it is the doer who finishes them. We are judged by our finished deeds, not by what we started. So, do not expect any miracles—make them happen!

Nowadays, a sense of urgency is a key part of the entrepreneur's culture. That is why you should *never leave for tomorrow that which you can do today*. Set your goals, your direction, your destination. Opportunity can only be seized by those who pursue it. Do not worry, get busy, because hard times will not last long, but people with strength endure.

Everyone wants to be an entrepreneur today, that is why competition is so fierce. The ground is fertile for all, although few will make it—there are too many of us. However, democratic access to global platforms, access to information, startups, incubators and accelerators, along with dissatisfaction with our present reality have all fertilized the ground for these new enterprises.

For me, an entrepreneur is the creator or originator of some type of innovating business opportunity, someone who studies and analyzes its possibilities, gathers resources, takes the risk, and who little by little gets the ball rolling along the road to materialize his dream.

Embarking on a project, like dreaming, is not only for the young, it is for everyone. Any one of us can decide to reinvent ourselves, or bring ideas to the table and solve the problems of the company we are working for. The more disruptive these projects are, the more value they add to improve life and enhance the world—with creativity, a positive attitude, and a fierce love for whatever one is embarking on—the closer we will be to attaining them.

«THE BEST WAY TO PREDICT THE FUTURE IS CREATING IT.»

ALAN KAY

To be good entrepreneurs, we need:

1. To love what we will be doing fiercely, enjoying the way we transform it into results.
2. To be positive.
3. To create a disruptive product or service.
4. To create a good quality product or service.
5. To persevere.
6. To be able to take risks and make the most of the opportunities we are afforded.

Most entrepreneurs have become so from practical xperience, like us, but one also learns by observing. A case in point are our colleagues, who every day watch and live how we make all our dreams come true at Xcaret, how our Dreamers generate ideas, how we evaluate them, and how the Board of Directors makes the decision of whether to take or not to take the risk.

Many entrepreneurs who are now important businessmen have emerged from our ranks, not to mention the many former colleagues who are now the heart and soul of our competitors.

So, take that leap of faith and let yourself be carried away by the wind. Do not take life too seriously. The best moment in life is exactly the one you are living. Love, laugh, cry, feel, dance, play, sing, taste, share, try, enjoy, produce, triumph, fall, and get back on your feet, over and over again, with passion!

ONE FOR THE ROAD

I have already shared with you, at the beginning of this story, how important my parents were in my education. I believe Xcaret reflects a lot of what they both taught me. I was privileged enough to have my mother living in the park during the last years of her life. Just like when I was a child, she kept teaching me so much, and correcting what she thought was wrong. Old habits die hard.

One day, during her morning walk through Xcaret, she came across a gardener who was pruning the plants. She watched him closely while he did his work, and with tender firmness pointed out that he was doing it wrong. The gardener, amazed, asked her what the proper way was, and delighted, she shared her knowledge with him. At the end, he thanked her for the lesson and asked her: «Are you the owner?» After a brief pause, she replied, holding her head up high: «No, I'm the owner's owner!» At our weekly family lunch, my mother told us this anecdote, and we subsequently referred to her that way. Today, the epitaph on her tombstone reads: «The owner's owner.»

Luis Miguel, my first-born, has always enjoyed going his own way, independently from the Group, doing his own supplying and leasing businesses—independently, yes, but never isolated. I have always counted on his talent for public relations and management when I have most needed them. He has become my right-hand, an extension of myself in complicated cases or very delicate ones requiring absolute trust. On the other hand, he is our purveyor of general or specialized products. I greatly admire his care and love for his children, being father, mother, and driver to them, 24/7. And, he is an xcellent planner of unique events.

As for David, he is my right-hand man in the construction business, and he leads the team of Dreamers. I am very demanding: with him, with Luis Miguel, and with any of my children who want to participate in the Group's projects. Certainly, they would have more chances to collaborate with me if they were not family, because I expect a lot, and I seem to be more demanding and stricter with them. It is part of the education I want to leave them. It does not mean I do not give them my support. But what I want is for them to make their own way, which they've done pretty well, so far.

My siblings, in spite of not being on the Group's payroll, have been an integral part of it since the beginning. They participate actively, serving as an extension of myself. Carlos is in charge of the monthly publication of the MAP-A and of its distribution in the airport and in car rental agencies. Rosi collaborates with everything that has to do with plants, orchids, and the gardens. She also handles a photographic archive of the Group's work. Guadalupe is director of the civil organization Flora, Fauna y Cultura de México, a social branch of the Group, handling several programs, including the turtle conservation, mangrove reforestation, community centers, and the La Ceiba park in Playa del Carmen. She is the founder of the Folk Art Museum (Museo de Arte Popular Mexicano) in Xcaret, and has been in charge of it since it was first created.

Marisol Marín Galera, my partner, has been my companion during my last adventures, now in Yucatán. Together, we go scouting for new places and products, looking for and developing artisans from all specialties. We discover new xenotes and supervise the ones under construction outside Quintana Roo.

My life has been divided into four exciting and beautiful chapters: Eva, Alma, Marisol Gallegos and Marisol Marín. Absolutely no regrets, and so much to be thankful for.

I would do it all over again, alongside these same wonderful companions.

For Mexico, I can only express my gratitude and admiration. It has given me everything. How I long to share how I feel with whoever I cross paths with! I would like to spread the love and admiration for my beautiful country, planted in me long ago, so that it grows in every one of my fellow citizens.

I always say that our parks have a mother and a father, because it is like taking care of a child. This is possible when there is continuity, the same head, a coherent idiosyncrasy, a DNA, a philosophy that can be followed and shared. For many years, I have been the negotiator and mediator among partners, and the provider of ideas for the concepts in the parks and attractions. That has been my main contribution. For as long as I live, God willing, I will continue to be the guiding thread, delegating responsibilities more and more, and keeping things up to date and efficient with new and young blood. We need to open our hearts and minds to change.

What I am looking for now is a new guiding thread to fit perfectly well with our endeavors, and for leadership that can offer continuity for years to come. The rules established in our Trust will facilitate this transition, they allow us to evolve by trying to ensure that each of our successors can grow, so they can be better than us.

Training and best practice allow us to create teams of xcellent leaders and loyal followers. Leaders with moral authority, not appointed by whim; people one can follow out of conviction, not because of the mere fact that they are our bosses. They must be empowered, trained in values and in how to use *that head of theirs* more and better, always looking for new and more efficient options, innovating, pursuing uniqueness, stretching our imagination and our creativity.

There is nothing we cannot imagine; imagination does not waste away, the more we use it, the more we have of it. The Group's growth depends on each colleague's growth, together we are more. We have already made more than 50 million visitors happy!

When you have a good team of colleagues who have fully embraced the company's DNA, who are team players and have the right role in the company, then you only need to guide them, because they will motivate each other, seeking their own self-fulfillment and development. You will not have to push them.

«I MUST FOLLOW THEM, FOR I AM THEIR LEADER.»

ANONYMOUS

I started Xcaret with a spirit of satisfaction derived from making it a reality, with a commitment to creativity, to beauty, to nature, and to quality. Back then, I was not thinking about the cost-benefit ratio. Nowadays, through the evolving spirit of the Group as a whole—company, colleagues, and visitors—we have reached a balance: between costs, benefits, budgets, possibilities, creativity, sustainability, and an increasing commitment to our country.

If I look back, and I see what we have achieved to date, I feel very proud. Xcaret keeps breaking new ground, and the best of all is that I keep being me: simple, meticulous, true to my word, intuitive, bold, easy-going, a timely trailblazer, sagacious, and positive. As if this description were not enough, if on any given day, while visiting Xcaret, you see a smiling, grizzled-haired man, picking up cigarette butts and trash, it is very likely you have found me. I would love to say hello to you.

I only hope that the Good Lord, my great family, my partners, my colleagues, and my friends remain at my side for a very long time, as they have until now, with so much love, sensitivity, health, and the capacity to be amazed.

Of course, the best is yet to come...

#ENTREPTIP:

The past is history; the future, a mystery; the present, a gift. Let us live it! Let us always do what we like best, otherwise, we will end up having to work.

Thank you to life

 What a Wonderful World Louis Armstrong

DECALOGUE

Make sure the things you do are one of a kind, and top of the line. **Innovation and imagination create opportunities, quality creates demand.**

We must surround ourselves with the best people; **an excellent human team is our greatest strength.**

Let us improve the development and well-being of our colleagues, their families, and the community. We must foster their improvement with good examples, knowledge, training, culture, sports, entertainment, benefits, and opportunities.

Things must be done right from the start. You'll never get a second chance to make a good first impression. **Excellence must be part of our routine.**

Creativity is a limitless resource. The more you use it, the more there is. **There is nothing we cannot imagine.**

Think globally, buy locally. Let us show solidarity with Mexico by consuming what the country produces.

Sustainability is not a choice, it is the right way. In nature, there are no rewards or punishments, only consequences.

#ENTREPT

We must banish **«it can't be done»** from our vocabulary and replace it with **«it can certainly be done».** We can do difficult straight away; impossible takes us a little longer.

No grand human enterprise has been accomplished with everyone's consent. You must have the courage to make decisions. **A single determined man makes a majority.**

The past is history; the future, a mystery; the present, a gift. Let us live it! **Let us always do what we like best, otherwise, we will end up having to work.**

2023

Great Little Hotels will open in Yucatán

2012

We were awarded the Ulysses prize by the World Tourism Organization

2022

The boutique hotel La Casa de la Playa is inagurated in December.

—

Construction work will begin on a huge natural park in the west of Yucatán

2013

We opened Xplor Fuego park

—

Tour Xenotes and Xoximilco park began operating

2021

Hotel Xcaret Arte is inagurated.

—

Xibalbá Reserve in Yucatán opens in December near Valladolid

2014

The Group's reengineering process began

2016

We opened Xenses park

COMING
SOON

2017

Hotel Xcaret México was inaugurated in December

2019

We opened Xavage park

HOTEL XCARET
MEXICO

XAVAGE
by xcaret

2018

Xcaret was granted the Liseberg Applause Award for «The Best Park in the World» by the IAAPA

1996

We began a sea turtle protection program in the Riviera Maya, with Xcaret's support

1998

We integrated the ball game played with the hips into the Xcaret México Espectacular show

1999

We introduced the all-inclusive park concept in Xel-Há

We opened Garrafón Park in Isla Mujeres, managed by Xcaret's founding partners.

2002

We opened the Gran Tlachco in Xcaret, México Espectacular show's new house
—
We began the Flora, Fauna y Cultura de México operation, the social and environmental branch of the Group

2008

The world financial crisis started in October
—
Our first General Director leaves

2007

We had our first Sacred Maya Journey Xcaret-Cozumel-Xcaret, sailing in wooden canoes.

2006

We sold Garrafón Park
—
The Festival of Life and Death was held for the first time in Xcaret. (Day of the Dead)

2005

Hurricane Emily (in July) and Wilma (in October) hit Cancún and the Riviera Maya

2009

I became the Group's General Director

The first outbreak of H1N1 influenza appears in April
—
We opened Xplor park in July

2010

We started operating tours to archaeological sites
—

A 100-year trust between partners was created

2003

We appointed our first ever General Director

1980

I bought and integrated Shop stores to the Pali chain

1978

I restructured the Diseño chain stores and renamed them Pali

HALF TIME

1985

I bought 12 acres to develop a residential complex in Xcaret and founded Promotora Xcaret S.A. de C.V.

1986

The Constandse brothers —Óscar, Marcos, and Carlos—joined the Xcaret project

1988

Hurricane Gilberto hit us and destroyed our recently built jetty, along with most of the vegetation

1990

Xcaret opened its doors to the public

1995

We began presenting Xcaret México Espectacular in July
—
Hurricane Roxanne visited our parks in October

1994

We opened Xel-Há park under the management of Xcaret's founding partners

1993

The scarlet macaw's reproduction program began

SECOND HALF

1992

I sold the Pali stores

1991

We finished the restoration work on the archaeological site in Polé, now Xcaret

Xel-Há
HIDDEN WONDER
by Xcaret

Xcaret!
by MEXICO

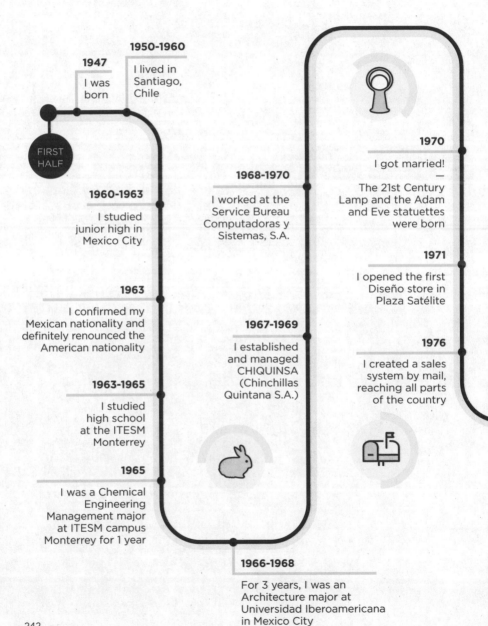

1947

I was born

1950-1960

I lived in Santiago, Chile

FIRST HALF

1960-1963

I studied junior high in Mexico City

1963

I confirmed my Mexican nationality and definitely renounced the American nationality

1963-1965

I studied high school at the ITESM Monterrey

1965

I was a Chemical Engineering Management major at ITESM campus Monterrey for 1 year

1966-1968

For 3 years, I was an Architecture major at Universidad Iberoamericana in Mexico City

1967-1969

I established and managed CHIQUINSA (Chinchillas Quintana S.A.)

1968-1970

I worked at the Service Bureau Computadoras y Sistemas, S.A.

1970

I got married!
—
The 21st Century Lamp and the Adam and Eve statuettes were born

1971

I opened the first Diseño store in Plaza Satélite

1976

I created a sales system by mail, reaching all parts of the country

Never risk your **family's assets** to embark
on a project.

Ideas must be sold, **not imposed**. You have
to be persuasive.

Do not underestimate your competitors, no
matter how small.

You must be open and transparent, but **not
reckless.**

Never sell to your competition if you are
competing in the same market.

Never relinquish control or split a shareholder
majority among so many partners that it
prevents you from making decisions and
timely investments.

Do not keep company with people who have
different goals to yours, a **different outlook
on** life, or worse, **different core values**.

Stay **straight**, become **exemplary**.

Being copied is a sign that you are on the **right track**.

Sustainability must be done over **360°** and in **third dimension**.

Those who have not embraced sustainability are destined to **disappear**.

For many people, success is about accumulating money; for others, it is about being famous; for me, it is about **achieving happiness**.

You do not have to be a millionaire **to be rich, just be generous**.

Learn to put your eggs in **different baskets**...and that **all baskets are important.**

If you're a baker, give away bread. When you share your own resources, the things you produce, it costs half as much and gives you twice the return.

Always include an **exit clause** whenever you seal a deal or sign a **contract.**

Listen to the market, but do not lose your core values, which are the reason why they prefer you. **Be creative and find solutions that are coherent with your philosophy.**

If you know where you are going, you **will get there faster.**

Ethics must always take precedence over efficiency, **principles** over results, **people** over things

Cash flow and **preparation** are the **lifesavers** in any crisis.

One must learn to calculate the risk, **test the waters**, and gradually move ahead.

Fortune visits us all, we must keep our eyes open to catch it. **Opportunities are never lost, only caught by another.**

You cannot win all wars. Have a clear goal, **focus on winning the main battles**, and be prepared to yield, tactically, on the smaller ones.

If someone buys, **sell**; if they sell, **buy**.

Travel, travel, travel. First, inside your own country; then, travel the world. You will see things you never imagined, you will learn things you did not know existed.

When selecting your target audience, try to be as inclusive as possible. **Design everything thinking about your clientes**: children, young people, and adults —they are all equally important.

Take **action today** for the **long run**.

Crises may be terrifying, but they can also present great opportunities. **Learn to read them. When everyone falls back, it is your chance to plough on.**

An entrepreneur **must listen to everyone**: his own conscience and the people around him. But in the end, **it is he who must make the decision.**

YOUR
CONCLUSIONS

....
....
....
....
....
....
....
....
....

There is a mailbox in my office where any colleague can let me know about their ideas or concerns.

If you want to, you can share with me what Xueños has inspired in you through my email address:

XuenosMiguel@xcaret.com

Xueños de Miguel Quintana Pali
se terminó de imprimir en marzo de 2023
en los talleres de
Litográfica Ingramex, S.A. de C.V.,
Centeno 162-1, Col. Granjas Esmeralda, C.P. 09810,
Ciudad de México.